D1000762

Library of Shakespearean Biography and Criticism

I. PRIMARY REFERENCE WORKS ON SHAKESPEARE

II. CRITICISM AND INTERPRETATION

    A. Textual Treatises, Commentaries
    B. Treatment of Special Subjects
    C. Dramatic and Literary Art in Shakespeare

III. SHAKESPEARE AND HIS TIME

    A. General Treatises. Biography
    B. The Age of Shakespeare
    C. Authorship

Series II, Part A

ROSALYNDE

LODGE'S 'ROSALYNDE' BEING THE ORIGINAL OF SHAKESPEARE'S 'AS YOU LIKE IT' EDITED BY W. W. GREG

Oneonta Public Library

BOOKS FOR LIBRARIES PRESS
FREEPORT, NEW YORK

Joe Namath - Gift

First Published 1907
Reprinted 1970

INTERNATIONAL STANDARD BOOK NUMBER:
0-8369-5510-2

LIBRARY OF CONGRESS CATALOG CARD NUMBER:
75-128890

PRINTED IN THE UNITED STATES OF AMERICA

INTRODUCTION

LODGE'S 'Rosalynde' has shared the fate of all books which have been the occasion of achievements greater than themselves. While its name has lived, along with those of a number of other works of more or less ephemeral interest and more or less secondary merit, as having supplied material for the consummate art of Shakespeare, little attention has ever been bestowed upon it for its own sake, and its own individual merits have been cast into the shade by the glory of its offspring. It has been treated merely as a source, as a thing of no value in itself; the interest it has aroused has been antiquarian rather than literary. Thus one class of Shakespearian editors dismiss it, along with other works in the same position, with some such facile remark as that Shakespeare's genius is nowhere more clearly seen than in the comparison of his work with his so-called sources; while others have patronized it with such injudicious praise as to commend its ' natural force and simplicity.' But such phrases have long ago returned upon the heads of those that coined them. Shakespeare's genius stands in no need of exaltation at the expense of those of his predecessors and contemporaries whose work he made his own, while nothing can be more grossly unfair than to subject such a work as ' Rosalynde ' to a comparison with such a one as ' As you Like it,' merely because Shakespeare's insight saw in the earlier work possibilities to which his less gifted editors have usually been blind.   Had it not been for the fact of Lodge's novel having furnished the dramatist with the outline—and a good deal more than the outline—of one of his most delightful comedies, its name would doubtless have figured less in the text books of English literature, but there would have been more chance of its receiving a genuinely critical appreciation.   Since, however, the fact remains that upon ' Rosalynde ' Shakespeare did found ' As you Like it,' the comparison of the two, not from the judicial but from the truly critical standpoint, becomes a matter of first-rate literary importance.   It is, however, a point belonging primarily to the criticism of Shakespeare and not of Lodge, and though it will be necessary to treat it at some length in the present introduction, it will first be necessary to consider the place occupied in the history of literature by ' Rosalynde ' itself, and the position it holds among its peers in the development of the English novel.

Pastoral Romance. The genus to which ' Rosalynde ' may most conveniently be referred, the pastoral romance, is one of respectable antiquity.   The earliest example of which we have knowledge is the famous ' Daphnis and Chloe,' a late Greek composition of the third century probably, by an author of the name of Longus.   This work became popular in the sixteenth century in the French translation by

Jacques Amyot, of which an English version by Angel Day appeared in 1587. It was, however, destined to remain in a somewhat solitary position and to exercise little influence upon the pastoral romance of later days. The work belonged to the school of so-called erotic romances, the majority of which were in no wise particularly pastoral. Moreover, though later writers appear to have been in many cases familiar with the work of Longus, and to have freely borrowed ideas and incidents, it was not from it that they received the impulse to pastoral creation, and neither continuity of tradition nor conscious discipleship connects the Greek romancier with his Italian successors. Longus himself appears to have been indebted to Theocritus for his pastoral inspiration and to have reproduced on Lesbian pastures the shepherd life of Sicily, and it is to Theocritus that we must return in seeking to trace out the history of pastoral tradition. The poetry of the Greek idylist, but feebly re-echoed in his immediate successors, rose once more to the first rank in literature, though under altered conditions and its character greatly changed, in the hands of Vergil. It was the form imposed on the tradition by the Roman poet that came to be venerated as classical in later ages, and the tradition left by him flowered once again in the first dawn of renaissance humanism. Petrarch composed Latin eclogues, and Boccaccio was proud to claim him as his master. Scarcely less important for the future of pastoralism than the tradition of the Vergilian eclogue, were the mythological legends such as supplied the subject of Ovid's 'Metamorphoses.'   As the new enthusiasm began to stir within the shell of medieval monasticism the woods and springs repeopled themselves with the awakened deities of earth, roguish fauns peered from amid the tangle of the copse, and the nymphs bathed once more in the freshness of the streams.   While Petrarch was directing the lash of the allegorical eclogue against the licence of the papal court at Avignon, Boccaccio was compiling, in his 'Genealogia Deorum,' the first mythological dictionary.   And it was from the admixture of these two related elements, pastoral and mythological, that there sprang the forerunner of the pastoral romance which flourished throughout the sixteenth century. This herald was Boccaccio's 'Ameto,' a medley of tales of a pastoral or mythological character in which the idyllic mode is attuned to a key of voluptuous languor, and in which the surcharged style affects us like the scent of hothouse lilies. The work has its interest to the student of Boccaccio and of Italian style, but for us its importance lies in the fact that it undoubtedly suggested to Sannazaro the form of his famous 'Arcadia' (1504).   It was this work that really initiated that ideal pastoral which exercised for centuries such a strange fascination over the minds of men, and, with more or less admixture of various kinds, added a new *genre* to all the principal literatures of Europe.   The 'Arcadia' is itself purely pastoral, the characters, however polished and refined, are genuine shepherd folk ; in no case does their pastoral guise cover the courtier or the priest, and there is no chivalric admixture. This latter was an addition which the original style received in Spain, where the kind was largely followed and developed, the most important example being Montemayor's 'Diana' and its continuations. As a development of the Spanish chivalric pastoral appeared later on the fashionable pastoral of France, as exemplified in D'Urfé's 'Astrée.' It was to Spain likewise that Sidney was indebted in the composition of the elaborate romance, which, however, he named after the original work of Sannazaro.

The first incomplete text of Sidney's 'Arcadia' appeared in 1590, the same year as 'Rosalynde.' Lodge may, of course, have seen the work, which circulated to some extent at least in manuscript, but the supposition is not forced upon us. Any general resemblance in the style of composition which exists, may be explained on the supposition of the author being acquainted with Montemayor's work, since he must almost certainly, one would think, have known Spanish. Moreover, the romance of adventure cast in a pastoral setting was by no means a novelty in literature. In English alone Greene's 'Menaphon' had appeared the year before 'Rosalynde,' while Lodge himself had made previous attempts in a somewhat similar line. The connection in style of Lodge's work with that of his friend Greene is far closer than with that of Sidney. In style and manner it is, of course, also connected with the work of Lyly, and through him may claim literary descent from another branch of Spanish literature. In this connection, however, it should be noted that Lodge's 'Rosalynde' presents no rustic characters corresponding to the Menaphon and Camilla of Greene, the Miso and Mopsa of Sidney—William and Audrey being among Shakespeare's additions to the cast. Lodge's debt to Lyly, however, or perhaps rather his desire to catch a little of the reflected glory of that writer's success, appears in the alternative title he adopted for his novel, 'Euphues' Golden Legacy.'

In considering the position occupied by 'Rosalynde' among works of the same class and of the same date it must be borne in mind that it has none of the historical importance attaching to 'Euphues,' nor does it enjoy any of the fortuitous advantages which make the appearance of Sidney's 'Arcadia' a landmark in English literature. This makes it difficult to estimate its real merit as compared with such works, though it may not be too bold to assert that it may claim to be far more entertaining than the first and far more complete and artistically balanced than the second. Such comparisons, however, are essentially uncritical and really beg the question ; if we are content to leave such works of extrinsic importance out of count, 'Rosalynde' has little to fear from a comparison with its peers. Certainly, as against such works as 'Menaphon' and 'Dorastus and Fawnia,' Lodge's novel can well hold its own. The standard of comparison may not be a high one—neither 'Rosalynde' nor 'Menaphon' belongs to great literature—but in its own particular style and within the limits of its kind the romance of Arden falls not far short of complete success. One must, however, be in the right mood to appreciate it. This, of course, is true of all literature and of all art generally, but it is a consideration of more than usual importance in such a case as this, in which the art has no force wherewith to compel the emotions, no power itself to create in the reader the right mood for its own enjoyment. No expectation of realism or of reality, no demand for powerful emotions or lofty idealism, must be allowed to interfere with the purely receptive state of mind. The reader must be prepared to accept the conventional sentiment, the stilted triviality, the prettiness and the pettiness of the style, with the same half-humorous seriousness with which the author wrote. For in spite of these characteristics, in spite of his proneness to the false school-rhetoric of the renaissance, there is a twitch about the corners of the author's mouth as he pens even his most solemn passages, and now and again he must needs laugh out for the mere fun of living, in defiance of every rule of courtly etiquette.

Thomas Lodge. The author of 'Rosalynde' was born about the year 1558. He came of a civic family of repute in London, his father, Sir Thomas Lodge, of the Grocers' Company, having filled the office of Lord Mayor in 1562–3, and his mother being the daughter of Sir William Laxton who had held the same dignity in 1544–5. He received his early education at Merchant Taylors' School and went to Oxford about 1573 as servitor of Edward Hoby, son of the translator of the 'Courtier,' then a

b

gentleman commoner at Trinity College. Lodge matriculated at the same college, became B.A. in 1577 and supplicated for the degree of M.A. in 1581, having been in the meanwhile admitted to Lincoln's Inn in 1578. In London he became intimate with Robert Greene, and soon found literature a more congenial occupation than the study of the law. He resolved to indulge his tastes in this direction, thereby incurring the loss of a certain legacy. The earliest literary effort of which we find any trace was an epitaph on his mother which was entered in December 1579, but of which nothing further is known. Early in 1580 appeared his first extant work, a 'Defence of Stage-Plays' in answer to Stephen Gosson's 'School of Abuse.' License was apparently refused, but the book circulated privately. Gosson replied to it in his 'Plays confuted in Five Actions' of 1582, and Lodge made a final retort in 1584 in a book called 'An Alarum against Usurers,' a work which may have been founded on his personal experience. Of his private affairs we know little, but he left a will dated 1583, from which we learn that he was already married at that date. At one time he had some connection with the stage. His play, 'The Wounds of Civil War,' printed in 1594, may have been produced in 1587. He also collaborated with Greene in 'A Looking-glass for London and England,' acted in 1592 and printed in 1594. All other dramatic attributions are hypothetical and of a very uncertain character. The romance and not the drama was to be Lodge's particular field. As

early as 1581 he revised by request Barnabe Rich's euphuistic romance entitled 'The Adventures of Don Simonides';
while his earliest original attempt, entitled 'The Delectable
History of Forbonius and Prisceria,' was published together
with the 'Alarum' in 1584. For a while he appears to
have followed the profession of arms, and about 1588 sailed to
the islands of Terceira and the Canaries with one Captain
Clarke. It was during this voyage that he wrote 'Rosalynde,' which was published in 1590. His first volume of
verse, a mythological tale entitled 'Scilla's Metamorphosis'
had appeared in 1589, and an historical romance on 'Robert,
Duke of Normandy,' was published early in 1591. In August
the same year he sailed with Cavendish for South America,
and visited Brazil and the Straits of Magellan. During his
absence Greene gave his friend's 'Euphues' Shadow' to the
press (1592) and after his return appeared his collection
of sonnets entitled 'Phillis' (1593). Other romances followed during the next three years, one of which, 'Margaret
of America,' purports to have been written in the Straits
of Magellan, and also some satires in verse under the title
of 'A Fig for Momus.' A religious tract, 'Prosopo-
poeia,' published in 1596, is Catholic in tone, and Lodge is
known to have joined the Roman communion in middle life.
He turned his attention to medicine, and according to Wood
graduated at Avignon in 1600. He was incorporated M.D.
at Oxford, October 25, 1602. The following year he published 'A treatise of the Plague.' With this exception the

last twenty-five years of his life were occupied with laborious
work on Josephus, Seneca and Du Bartas. He died in
1625.

Sources of ' Rosalynde ' and its relation to ' As you Like it.'

In writing ' Rosalynde ' Lodge undoubtedly
made use of the Middle English tale of Gamelyn, a poem
interesting in more ways than one. It is a composition of
the middle of the fourteenth century probably, and has come
down to us in several manuscripts of Chaucer's ' Canterbury
Tales.' In spite of this fact it is undoubtedly not by Chaucer,
but may have been among his materials, and it has been not
improbably conjectured that it was intended to be worked up
into the Yeoman's tale. As the poem was not included in
any of the black-letter editions of Chaucer, Lodge must have
become acquainted with it in manuscript. This source supplied
Lodge with the story of Sir John of Bordeaux and his three
sons, the adventure of the hero in the wrestling at court, and
his escape into the forest, where he joins a band of outlaws.
The rest of the story, and even much of the detail of the
earlier part, bears no resemblance to Lodge's work, nor is
there any mention of a woman in the whole poem till we come
to within a few lines of the end, where we are informed that
Gamelyn ' wedded a wife both good and fair.' It is therefore but a very partial source of ' Rosalynde.' Whether
Lodge had any other original is not known. It has been
conjectured that the more important portion of the story is
based on some Italian novel, but as yet none such has been

discovered. Nor is the suggestion on the whole very likely. It is much more probable that a writer starting with the tale of the outlawed youth should expand and complete it by the invention of its counterpart in which the protagonist should be a princess, than that he should accidentally come across and piece together two such closely related tales. Rosalynde and Alinda, the banished duke and his usurping brother, the proud Phoebe and lovesick Montanus, may be in all likelihood set down to the invention of the romancier and the inspiration of the Canaries. Of course it is perfectly possible that certain incidents may have been borrowed from, and certain characters suggested by, earlier works. The plot of the novel as we have it has points of resemblance with the tale of Havelok; the proud shepherdess and lovelorn swain and the girl in page's attire were already traditional. But for those fundamental outlines of the story which enabled it to be woven into a harmonious whole with the Middle English tale, Lodge must almost of necessity have been responsible.

While Lodge was indebted to earlier work for a comparatively insignificant portion only of his plot, we have in 'Rosalynde' practically the perfect outline and groundwork of 'As you Like it.' The story in itself as we know it, apart from its dramatic presentation, is the work of Lodge. There are, of course, points of difference in plot and dissimilarity in the characters between the romance and the drama, but as regards the formal skeleton, so to speak, they are of comparative unimportance. They will be obvious to any one who, with a recollection of Shakespeare's work, will read the present novel. Some of the changes may be traced to the difference between the modes of presentation, narrative and dramatic, others to the dramatist's artistic tact. There is difference again in the style, for the romance is strongly euphuistic in tone and mannered in expression, of which hardly a touch remains in the play. It is true that some of the lyrical passages of the latter remind us by their conscious artificiality of Lodge's less inspired attempts, but this is intentional and deliberately calculated to attract attention by contrast with the rest of the composition. It is also true that, in his songs, Lodge repeatedly led off with a burst of melody and vigorous execution. Had the description of Rosalynde (p. 70) for instance fulfilled the promise of the first two lines, it would have been one of the most gorgeous poems in the language. He even now and again achieved a sustained success, though he seldom produced such wholly delightful verses as Rosalynde's madrigal (p. 27). Shakespeare, on the other hand, commanded with the careless ease of a master every stop upon the pipe of song, and could from each draw forth its perfect and proper melody. Again, while leaving the plot unaffected, Shakespeare made some not unimportant additions to the dramatis personae. Besides certain minor characters, we owe to him Jaques, Touchstone, William and Audrey. That much of the delight of the play depends upon the first two, although neither sustains any essential part in the piece, may be freely allowed. The introduction of the last two appears to have been the result of a deliberate plan. It would seem as if, by placing side by side the masquerading court pastoralism of the main plot, the refined Arcadian tradition to which we owe Phoebe and Sylvius, and the boorish if sympathetic rusticity of his addition to the cast, Shakespeare intended to bring the whole graceful figment to the touchstone of reality and hint at the instability of the ideal and convention of which he nevertheless made use. That he should do this while investing it with all the seduction of his most consummate art is in perfect keeping with the character of his genius. He could afford to do so, for he never treated the convention under which he worked, or which he chose to adopt, with that distressing seriousness into which pastoral writers in particular were constantly liable to fall. With him the form is more or less a matter of indifference, the value of his characters depends, not upon the conventional type to which they happen to belong, but upon their underlying humanity. In Lodge it is true that we occasionally, as it were, surprise a character breaking through the shell of its conventional artificiality with a touch of genuine humour or common human nature, but it is in Shakespeare alone that under whatever form they may appear the characters are always and for ever fellow human beings with ourselves. All those formal differences between the romance of ' Rosalynde ' and ' As you Like it ' noticed above, and a great deal more, less susceptible of precise statement but not therefore less important, is included in the general state-

ment that the differences between the two are such as must
of necessity exist between the work of Shakespeare in the
full maturity of his genius and that of any respectable scribbler
such as Lodge. And this brings me back to the point with
which I started, the futile injustice, namely, of basing any
judicial criticism upon a comparison of the two. 'Rosalynde'
belongs to one sphere of literature, 'As you Like it' to
another, in spite of the fact that a study of both may be
necessary to the just understanding of either, and of the
conditions under which they were alike produced. A cottage may be none the less delightful for not being a castle,
even though the historian may point out the architectural
connection between them.

Text. On Oct. 6, 1590, 'Rosalynde' was entered on
the Stationers' Register to Nicholas Ling and John Busby.
The two earliest editions were published by the latter in
1590 and 1592 respectively. Of the earlier of these the
only known copy, unluckily wanting one sheet, is in private
hands; of the later two copies are among Malone's books
at the Bodleian and a third again in a private library. Later
editions appeared in 1598, 1604, 1609, 1612, 1614, 1623-4,
1634 and 1642.

In the present reprint the spelling has been modernized—
a reprehensible practice—except in the case of a few words
which I could not bring myself to sacrifice. The general
system of punctuation and paragraphing has also been com-

pletely modified, and an attempt has been made to give the work the benefit of such adventitious aids to style as typography can supply, aids which are sadly lacking in the old editions. If in doing so I have ever misinterpreted my author's meaning, which is possible, I must crave forgiveness of his ghost. The reader will, I think, find the change tend to his convenience. In the notes I have recorded the variations of reading between the two earliest editions. For those of the quarto of 1592 I have had the opportunity of consulting the copies at Oxford; for those of the quarto of 1590 I have relied on the apparently very accurate reprint issued by the Hunterian Club of Glasgow in 1878. The glossary will explain a few unusual words and serve as an index to the allusions. As an appendix has also been added Mr. Stone's study of the relation of 'As you Like it' to 'Rosalynde,' originally published in the Transactions of the New Shakspere Society.

Rosalynde.

Euphues golden le-

gacie: found after his death
in his Cell at Si-
lexedra.

Bequeathed to Philautus fonnes
nourfed vp with their
father in Eng-
land.

Fetcht from the Canaries.
By T. L. Gent.

[Orwin's device with the motto: 'By Wisdome
Peace, By Peace Plenty.']

L O N D O N,
Imprinted by *Thomas Orwin* for *T. G.*
and *John Busbie.*
1 5 9 0.

To the Right Honourable and his most esteemed Lord the Lord of Hunsdon, Lord Chamberlain to her Majesty's Household, and Governor of her Town of Berwick : T. L. G. wisheth increase of all honourable virtues.

SUCH Romans, right honourable, as delighted in martial exploits, attempted their actions in the honour of Augustus, because he was a patron of soldiers : and Vergil dignified him with his poems, as a Maecenas of scholars ; both jointly advancing his royalty, as a prince warlike and learned. Such as sacrifice to Pallas present her with bays as she is wise, and with armour as she is valiant ; observing herein that excellent τὸ πρέπον, which dedicateth honours according to the perfection of the person. When I entered, right honourable, with a deep insight into the consideration of these premises, seeing your Lordship to be a patron of all martial men, and a Maecenas of such as apply themselves to study, wearing with Pallas both the lance and the bay, and aiming with Augustus at the favour of all, by the honourable virtues of your mind, being myself first a student, and after falling from books to arms, even vowed in all my thoughts dutifully to affect your Lordship. Having with Captain Clarke made a voyage to the island of Terceras and the Canaries, to beguile the time with labour I writ this book ; rough, as hatched in the storms of the ocean, and feathered in the surges of many perilous seas. But as it is the work of a soldier and a scholar, I presumed to shroud it under your Honour's patronage, as one that is the fautor and favourer of all virtuous actions ; and whose honourable loves, grown from the general applause of the whole commonwealth for your higher deserts, may keep it from the malice of every bitter tongue. Other reasons more particular, right honourable, challenge in me a special affection to your Lordship, as being a scholar with your two noble sons, Master Edmund Carew, and Master Robert Carew, two scions worthy of so honourable a tree, and a tree glorious in such honourable fruit, as also being scholar in the university under that learned and virtuous knight Sir Edward Hoby, when he was Bachelor in Arts, a man as well lettered as well born, and, after the etymology of his name, soaring as high as the wings of knowledge can mount him, happy every way, and the more fortunate, as blessed in the honour of so virtuous a lady. Thus, right honourable, the duty that I owe to the sons, chargeth me that all my affection be placed on the father; for where the branches are so precious, the tree of force must be most excellent. Commanded and emboldened thus with the consideration of these forepassed reasons, to present my book to your Lordship, I humbly entreat your

Honour will vouch of my labours, and favour a soldier's and a scholar's pen with your gracious acceptance, who answers in affection what he wants in eloquence; so devoted to your honour, as his only desire is, to end his life under the favour of so martial and learned a patron.

Resting thus in hope of your Lordship's courtesy in deigning the patronage of my work, I cease, wishing you as many honourable fortunes as your Lordship can desire or I imagine.

Your Honour's soldier
humbly affectionate:
Thomas Lodge.

TO THE GENTLEMEN READERS

GENTLEMEN, look not here to find any sprigs of Pallas'
bay tree, nor to hear the humour of any amorous laureate,
nor the pleasing vein of any eloquent orator: *Nolo altum
sapere*, they be matters above my capacity: the cobbler's
check shall never light on my head, *Ne sutor ultra crepi-
dam;* I will go no further than the latchet, and then all is
well. Here you may perhaps find some leaves of Venus'
myrtle, but hewn down by a soldier with his curtal-axe, not
bought with the allurement of a filed tongue. To be brief,
gentlemen, room for a soldier and a sailor, that gives you
the fruits of his labours that he wrote in the ocean, when
every line was wet with a surge, and every humorous passion
counterchecked with a storm. If you like it, so ; and yet I
will be yours in duty, if you be mine in favour. But it
Momus or any squint-eyed ass, that hath mighty ears to conceive with Midas, and yet little reason to judge, if he come
aboard our bark to find fault with the tackling, when he
knows not the shrouds, I'll down into the hold, and fetch
out a rusty pole-axe, that saw no sun this seven year, and
either well baste him, or heave the cockscomb overboard
to feed cods. But courteous gentlemen, that favour most,
backbite none, and pardon what is overslipped, let such come
and welcome ; I'll into the steward's room, and fetch them
a can of our best beverage. Well, gentlemen, you have
Euphues' Legacy. I fetched it as far as the island of
Terceras, and therefore read it : censure with favour, and
farewell   Yours,   T. L.

THE SCHEDULE ANNEXED TO EUPHUES' TESTAMENT, THE
TENOR OF HIS LEGACY, THE TOKEN OF HIS LOVE

THE vehemency of my sickness, Philautus, hath made
me doubtful of life, yet must I die in counselling thee like
Socrates, because I love thee. Thou hast sons by Camilla,
as I hear, who being young in years have green thoughts,
and nobly born have great minds : bend them in their youth
like the willow, lest thou bewail them in their age for their
wilfulness. I have bequeathed them a golden legacy, because
I greatly love thee. Let them read it as Archelaus did
Cassender, to profit by it ; and in reading let them meditate,
for I have approved it the best method. They shall find
Love anatomized by Euphues with as lively colours as in
Apelles' table: roses to whip him when he is wanton,
reasons to withstand him when he is wily. Here may
they read that virtue is the king of labours, opinion the
mistress of fools ; that unity is the pride of nature, and con-
tention the overthrow of families : here is elleborus, bitter
in taste, but beneficial in trial. I have nothing to send thee
and Camilla but this counsel, that instead of worldly goods
you leave your sons virtue and glory ; for better were they to
be partakers of your honours than lords of your manors.
I feel death that summoneth me to my grave, and my soul
desirous of his God. Farewell, Philautus, and let the
tenor of my counsel be applied to thy children's comfort.

Euphues dying to live.

If any man find this scroll, send it to Philautus in England.

ROSALYNDE

THERE dwelled adjoining to the city of Bordeaux a
knight of most honourable parentage, whom fortune
had graced with many favours, and nature honoured with
sundry exquisite qualities, so beautified with the excellence
of both, as it was a question whether fortune or nature
were more prodigal in deciphering the riches of their
bounties. Wise he was, as holding in his head a supreme
conceit of policy, reaching with Nestor into the depth of all
civil government; and to make his wisdom more gracious,
he had that *salem ingenii* and pleasant eloquence that was so
highly commended in Ulysses: his valour was no less than
his wit, nor the stroke of his lance no less forcible than
the sweetness of his tongue was persuasive; for he was for
his courage chosen the principal of all the Knights of Malta.
This hardy knight, thus enriched with virtue and honour,
surnamed Sir John of Bordeaux, having passed the prime of
his youth in sundry battles against the Turks, at last, as the
date of time hath his course, grew aged. His hairs were
silver-hued, and the map of age was figured on his forehead:
honour sat in the furrows of his face, and many years were

B

portrayed in his wrinkled lineaments, that all men might perceive his glass was run, and that nature of necessity challenged her due. Sir John, that with the Phoenix knew the term of his life was now expired, and could, with the swan, discover his end by her songs, having three sons by his wife Lynida, the very pride of all his forepassed years, thought now, seeing death by constraint would compel him to leave them, to bestow upon them such a legacy as might bewray his love, and increase their ensuing amity. Calling, therefore, these young gentlemen before him, in the presence of all his fellow Knights of Malta, he resolved to leave them a memorial of all his fatherly care in setting down a method of their brotherly duties. Having, therefore, death in his looks to move them to pity, and tears in his eyes to paint out the depth of his passions, taking his eldest son by the hand, he began thus :

' O my sons, you see that fate hath set a period of my years, and destinies have determined the final end of my days: the palm tree waxeth away-ward, for he stoopeth in his height, and my plumes are full of sick feathers touched with age. I must to my grave that dischargeth all cares, and leave you to the world that increaseth many sorrows : my silver hairs containeth great experience, and in the number of my years are penned down the subtleties of fortune. Therefore, as I leave you some fading pelf to countercheck poverty, so I will bequeath you infallible precepts that shall

Sir John of Bordeaux' legacy he gave to his sons.

lead you unto virtue. First, therefore, unto thee Saladyne, the eldest, and therefore the chiefest pillar of my house, wherein should be engraven as well the excellence of thy father's qualities, as the essential form of his proportion, to thee I give fourteen ploughlands, with all my manor houses and richest plate. Next, unto Fernandyne I bequeath twelve ploughlands. But, unto Rosader, the youngest, I give my horse, my armour, and my lance, with sixteen ploughlands ; for if the inward thoughts be discovered by outward shadows, Rosader will exceed you all in bounty and honour. Thus, my sons, have I parted in your portions the substance of my wealth, wherein if you be as prodigal to spend as I have been careful to get, your friends will grieve to see you more wasteful than I was bountiful, and your foes smile that my fall did begin in your excess. Let mine honour be the glass of your actions, and the fame of my virtues the lode-star to direct the course of your pilgrimage. Aim your deeds by my honourable endeavours, and show yourselves scions worthy of so flourishing a tree, lest, as the birds Halcyones, which exceed in whiteness, I hatch young ones that surpass in blackness. Climb not, my sons : aspiring pride is a vapour that ascendeth high, but soon turneth to a smoke ; they which stare at the stars stumble upon stones, and such as gaze at the sun, unless they be eagle-eyed, fall blind. Soar not with the hobby, lest you fall with the lark, nor attempt not with Phaeton, lest you drown with Icarus. Fortune, when she wills you to fly, tempers your plumes with wax; and therefore either sit still and make no wing, or else beware the sun, and hold Daedalus' axiom authentical, *medium tenere tutissimum.* Low shrubs have deep roots, and poor cottages great patience. Fortune looks ever upward, and envy aspireth to nestle with dignity. Take heed, my sons, the mean is sweetest melody; where strings high stretched, either soon crack, or quickly grow out of tune. Let your country's care be your heart's content, and think that you are not born for yourselves, but to level your thoughts to be loyal to your prince, careful for the common weal, and faithful to your friends; so shall France say, "These men are as excellent in virtues as they be exquisite in features." O my sons, a friend is a precious jewel, within whose bosom you may unload your sorrows and unfold your secrets, and he either will relieve with counsel, or persuade with reason; but take heed in the choice: the outward show makes not the inward man, nor are the dimples in the face the calendars of truth. When the liquorice leaf looketh most dry, then it is most wet: when the shores of Lepanthus are most quiet, then they forepoint a storm. The Baaran leaf the more fair it looks, the more infectious it is, and in the sweetest words is oft hid the most treachery. Therefore, my sons, choose a friend as the Hyperborei do the metals, sever them from the ore with fire, and let them not bide the stamp before they be current: so try and then trust, let time be touch-stone of friendship, and then friends faithful lay them up for

jewels. Be valiant, my sons, for cowardice is the enemy to
honour; but not too rash, for that is an extreme. Fortitude
is the mean, and that is limited within bonds, and prescribed
with circumstance. But above all,' and with that he fetched
a deep sigh, 'beware of love, for it is far more perilous
than pleasant, and yet, I tell you, it allureth as ill as the
Sirens. O my sons, fancy is a fickle thing, and beauty's
paintings are tricked up with time's colours, which, being set
to dry in the sun, perish with the same. Venus is a wanton,
and though her laws pretend liberty, yet there is nothing but
loss and glistering misery. Cupid's wings are plumed with
the feathers of vanity, and his arrows, where they pierce,
enforce nothing but deadly desires: a woman's eye, as it is
precious to behold, so is it prejudicial to gaze upon; for as it
affordeth delight, so it snareth unto death. Trust not their
fawning favours, for their loves are like the breath of a man
upon steel, which no sooner lighteth on but it leapeth off,
and their passions are as momentary as the colours of a
polype, which changeth at the sight of every object. My
breath waxeth short, and mine eyes dim: the hour is come,
and I must away; therefore let this suffice: women are
wantons, and yet men cannot want one: and therefore, if you
love, choose her that hath eyes of adamant, that will turn
only to one point; her heart of a diamond, that will receive
but one form; her tongue of a Sethin leaf, that never wags
but with a south-east wind: and yet, my sons, if she have all
these qualities, to be chaste, obedient, and silent, yet for that

she is a woman, shalt thou find in her sufficient vanities to countervail her virtues. Oh now, my sons, even now take these my last words as my latest legacy, for my thread is spun, and my foot is in the grave. Keep my precepts as memorials of your father's counsels, and let them be lodged in the secret of your hearts ; for wisdom is better than wealth, and a golden sentence worth a world of treasure. In my fall see and mark, my sons, the folly of man, that being dust climbeth with Biares to reach at the heavens, and ready every minute to die, yet hopeth for an age of pleasures. Oh, man's life is like lightning that is but a flash, and the longest date of his years but as a bavin's blaze. Seeing then man is so mortal, be careful that thy life be virtuous, that thy death may be full of admirable honours : so shalt thou challenge fame to be thy fautor, and put oblivion to exile with thine honourable actions. But, my sons, lest you should forget your father's axioms, take this scroll, wherein read what your father dying wills you to execute living.' At this he shrunk down in his bed, and gave up the ghost.

John of Bordeaux being thus dead was greatly lamented of his sons, and bewailed of his friends, especially of his fellow Knights of Malta, who attended on his funerals, which were performed with great solemnity. His obsequies done, Saladyne caused, next his epitaph, the contents of the scroll to be portrayed out, which were to this effect :

THE CONTENTS OF THE SCHEDULE WHICH SIR JOHN OF BORDEAUX GAVE TO HIS SONS

My sons, behold what portion I do give:
  I leave you goods, but they are quickly lost;
I leave advice, to school you how to live;
  I leave you wit, but won with little cost;
But keep it well, for counsel still is one,
When father, friends, and worldly goods are gone.

In choice of thrift let honour be thy gain,
  Win it by virtue and by manly might;
In doing good esteem thy toil no pain;
  Protect the fatherless and widow's right:
Fight for thy faith, thy country, and thy king,
For why? this thrift will prove a blessèd thing.

In choice of wife, prefer the modest-chaste;
  Lilies are fair in show, but foul in smell:
The sweetest looks by age are soon defaced;
  Then choose thy wife by wit and living well.
Who brings thee wealth and many faults withal,
Presents thee honey mixed with bitter gall.

In choice of friends, beware of light belief;
  A painted tongue may shroud a subtle heart;
The Siren's tears do threaten mickle grief;
  Foresee, my sons, for fear of sudden smart:
Choose in thy wants, and he that friends thee then,
When richer grown, befriend thou him agen.

Learn with the ant in summer to provide;
  Drive with the bee the drone from out thy hive:
Build like the swallow in the summer tide;
  Spare not too much, my sons, but sparing thrive:

Be poor in folly, rich in all but sin :
So by thy death thy glory shall begin.

Saladyne having thus set up the schedule, and hanged about
his father's hearse many passionate poems, that France might
suppose him to be passing sorrowful, he clad himself and
his brothers all in black, and in such sable suits discoursed
his grief: but as the hyena when she mourns is then most
guileful, so Saladyne under this show of grief shadowed a
heart full of contented thoughts. The tiger, though he
hide his claws, will at last discover his rapine : the lion's looks
are not the maps of his meaning, nor a man's physnomy is
not the display of his secrets. Fire cannot be hid in the straw,
nor the nature of man so concealed, but at last it will have
his course : nurture and art may do much, but that *natura
naturans*, which by propagation is ingrafted in the heart, will
be at last perforce predominant according to the old verse :

Naturam expellas furca, tamen usque recurret.

So fared it with Saladyne, for after a month's mourning was
passed, he fell to consideration of his father's testament ; how
he had bequeathed more to his younger brothers than himself, that Rosader was his father's darling, but now under
his tuition, that as yet they were not come to years, and he
being their guardian, might, if not defraud them of their due,
yet make such havoc of their legacies and lands, as they
should be a great deal the lighter : whereupon he began thus
to meditate with himself:

' Saladyne, how art thou disquieted in thy thoughts, and perplexed with a world of restless passions, having thy mind troubled with the tenor of thy father's testament, *Saladyne's* and thy heart fired with the hope of present *meditation* preferment ! By the one thou art counselled to *with himself.* content thee with thy fortunes, by the other persuaded to aspire to higher wealth. Riches, Saladyne, is a great royalty, and there is no sweeter physic than store. Avicen, like a fool, forgot in his Aphorisms to say that gold was the most precious restorative, and that treasure was the most excellent medicine of the mind. O Saladyne, what, were thy father's precepts breathed into the wind? hast thou so soon forgotten his principles? did he not warn thee from coveting without honour, and climbing without virtue? did he not forbid thee to aim at any action that should not be honourable? and what will be more prejudicial to thy credit, than the careless ruin of thy brothers' welfare? why, shouldst not thou be the pillar of thy brothers' prosperity? and wilt thou become the subversion of their fortunes? is there any sweeter thing than concord, or a more precious jewel than amity? are you not sons of one father, scions of one tree, birds of one nest, and wilt thou become so unnatural as to rob them, whom thou shouldst relieve? No, Saladyne, entreat them with favours, and entertain them with love, so shalt thou have thy conscience clear and thy renown excellent. Tush, what words are these, base fool, far unfit, if thou be wise, for thy humour? What though thy father at his

death talked of many frivolous matters, as one that doated for
age and raved in his sickness; shall his words be axioms, and
his talk be so authentical, that thou wilt, to observe them,
prejudice thyself? No no, Saladyne, sick men's wills that
are parole and have neither hand nor seal, are like the
laws of a city written in dust, which are broken with the
blast of every wind. What, man, thy father is dead, and
he can neither help thy fortunes, nor measure thy actions;
therefore bury his words with his carcase, and be wise for
thyself. What, 'tis not so old as true,

> Non sapit, qui sibi non sapit.

Thy brother is young, keep him now in awe; make him
not checkmate with thyself, for

> Nimia familiaritas contemptum parit.

Let him know little, so shall he not be able to execute
much: suppress his wits with a base estate, and though he be
a gentleman by nature, yet form him anew, and make him a
peasant by nurture: so shalt thou keep him as a slave, and
reign thyself sole lord over all thy father's possessions.
As for Fernandyne, thy middle brother, he is a scholar and
hath no mind but on Aristotle: let him read on Galen
while thou riflest with gold, and pore on his book till thou
dost purchase lands: wit is great wealth; if he have learning
it is enough: and so let all rest.'

In this humour was Saladyne, making his brother Rosader
his foot-boy, for the space of two or three years, keeping

him in such servile subjection, as if he had been the son
of any country vassal. The young gentleman bore all with
patience, till on a day, walking in the garden by himself, he
began to consider how he was the son of John of Bordeaux, a knight renowmed for many victories, and a gentleman famosed for his virtues ; how, contrary to the testament
of his father, he was not only kept from his land and entreated as a servant, but smothered in such secret slavery, as
he might not attain to any honourable actions.

' Ah,' quoth he to himself, nature working these effectual
passions, ' why should I, that am a gentleman born, pass
my time in such unnatural drudgery ? were it not better
either in Paris to become a scholar, or in the court a courtier,
or in the field a soldier, than to live a foot-boy to my own
brother ? Nature hath lent me wit to conceive, but my brother
denied me art to contemplate : I have strength to perform
any honourable exploit, but no liberty to accomplish my
virtuous endeavours : those good parts that God hath bestowed
upon me, the envy of my brother doth smother in obscurity ;
the harder is my fortune, and the more his frowardness.'

With that casting up his hand he felt hair on his face,
and perceiving his beard to bud, for choler he began to
blush, and swore to himself he would be no more subject to
such slavery. As thus he was ruminating of his melancholy
passions in came Saladyne with his men, and seeing his
brother in a brown study, and to forget his wonted reverence,
thought to shake him out of his dumps thus :

'Sirrah,' quoth he, 'what is your heart on your halfpenny, or are you saying a dirge for your father's soul? What, is my dinner ready?'

At this question Rosader, turning his head askance, and bending his brows as if anger there had ploughed the furrows of her wrath, with his eyes full of fire, he made this reply:

'Dost thou ask me, Saladyne, for thy cates? ask some of thy churls who are fit for such an office: I am thine equal by nature, though not by birth, and though thou hast more cards in the bunch, I have as many trumps in my hands as thyself. Let me question with thee, why thou hast felled my woods, spoiled my manor houses, and made havoc of such utensils as my father bequeathed unto me? I tell thee, Saladyne, either answer me as a brother, or I will trouble thee as an enemy.'

At this reply of Rosader's Saladyne smiled as laughing at his presumption, and frowned as checking his folly: he therefore took him up thus shortly:

'What, sirrah! well I see early pricks the tree that will prove a thorn: hath my familiar conversing with you made you coy, or my good looks drawn you to be thus contemptuous? I can quickly remedy such a fault, and I will bend the tree while it is a wand. In faith, sir boy, I have a snaffle for such a headstrong colt. You, sirs, lay hold on him and bind him, and then I will give him a cooling card for his choler.'

This made Rosader half mad, that stepping to a great rake that stood in the garden, he laid such load upon his brother's men that he hurt some of them, and made the rest of them run away. Saladyne, seeing Rosader so resolute and with his resolution so valiant, thought his heels his best safety, and took him to a loft adjoining to the garden, whither Rosader pursued him hotly. Saladyne, afraid of his brother's fury, cried out to him thus:

'Rosader, be not so rash: I am thy brother and thine elder, and if I have done thee wrong I'll make thee amends: revenge not anger in blood, for so shalt thou stain the virtue of old Sir John of Bordeaux. Say wherein thou art discontent and thou shalt be satisfied. Brothers' frowns ought not to be periods of wrath: what, man, look not so sourly; I know we shall be friends, and better friends than we have been, for, *Amantium ira amoris redintegratio est.*'

These words appeased the choler of Rosader, for he was of a mild and courteous nature, so that he laid down his weapons, and upon the faith of a gentleman assured his brother he would offer him no prejudice: whereupon Saladyne came down, and after a little parley they embraced each other and became friends; and Saladyne promising Rosader the restitution of all his lands, 'and what favour else,' quoth he, 'any ways my ability or the nature of a brother may perform.' Upon these sugared reconciliations they went into the house arm in arm together, to the great content of all the old servants of Sir John of Bordeaux.

Thus continued the pad hidden in the straw, till it chanced that Torismond, king of France, had appointed for his pleasure a day of wrastling and of tournament to busy his commons' heads, lest, being idle, their thoughts should run upon more serious matters, and call to remembrance their old banished king. A champion there was to stand against all comers, a Norman, a man of tall stature and of great strength; so valiant, that in many such conflicts he always bare away the victory, not only overthrowing them which he encountered, but often with the weight of his body killing them outright. Saladyne hearing of this, thinking now not to let the ball fall to the ground, but to take opportunity by the forehead, first by secret means convented with the Norman, and procured him with rich rewards to swear that if Rosader came within his claws he should never more return to quarrel with Saladyne for his possessions. The Norman desirous of pelf—as *Quis nisi mentis inops oblatum respuit aurum ?*—taking great gifts for little gods, took the crowns of Saladyne to perform the stratagem.

Having thus the champion tied to his villainous determination by oath, he prosecuted the intent of his purpose thus. He went to young Rosader, who in all his thoughts reached at honour, and gazed no lower than virtue commanded him, and began to tell him of this tournament and wrastling, how the king should be there, and all the chief peers of France, with all the beautiful damosels of the country.

'Now, brother,' quoth he, 'for the honour of Sir John

of Bordeaux, our renowmed father, to famous that house
that never hath been found without men approved in
chivalry, show thy resolution to be peremptory. For
myself thou knowest, though I am eldest by birth, yet
never having attempted any deeds of arms, I am youngest
to perform any martial exploits, knowing better how to
survey my lands than to charge my lance : my brother
Fernandyne he is at Paris poring on a few papers, having
more insight into sophistry and principles of philosophy,
than any warlike endeavours ; but thou, Rosader, the
youngest in years but the eldest in valour, art a man of
strength, and darest do what honour allows thee. Take
thou my father's lance, his sword, and his horse, and hie
thee to the tournament, and either there valiantly crack a
spear, or try with the Norman for the palm of activity.'

The words of Saladyne were but spurs to a free horse,
for he had scarce uttered them, ere Rosader took him in
his arms, taking his proffer so kindly, that he promised in
what he might to requite his courtesy. The next morrow
was the day of the tournament, and Rosader was so desirous
to show his heroical thoughts that he passed the night with
little sleep ; but as soon as Phoebus had vailed the curtain of
the night, and made Aurora blush with giving her the *bezo les
labres* in her silver couch, he gat him up, and taking his leave
of his brother, mounted himself towards the place appointed,
thinking every mile ten leagues till he came there.

But leaving him so desirous of the journey, to Torismond,

the king of France, who having by force banished Gerismond, their lawful king, that lived as an outlaw in the forest of Arden, sought now by all means to keep the French busied with all sports that might breed their content. Amongst the rest he had appointed this solemn tournament, whereunto he in most solemn manner resorted, accompanied with the twelve peers of France, who, rather for fear than love, graced him with the show of their dutiful favours. To feed their eyes, and to make the beholders pleased with the sight of most rare and glistering objects, he had appointed his own daughter Alinda to be there, and the fair Rosalynde, daughter unto Gerismond, with all the beautiful damosels that were famous for their features in all France. Thus in that place did love and war triumph in a sympathy; for such as were martial might use their lance to be renowmed for the excellence of their chivalry, and such as were amorous might glut themselves with gazing on the beauties of most heavenly creatures. As every man's eye had his several survey, and fancy was partial in their looks, yet all in general applauded the admirable riches that nature bestowed on the face of Rosalynde; for upon her cheeks there seemed a battle between the Graces, who should bestow most favours to make her excellent. The blush that gloried Luna, when she kissed the shepherd on the hills of Latmos, was not tainted with such a pleasant dye as the vermilion flourished on the silver hue of Rosalynde's countenance: her eyes were like those lamps that make the wealthy covert of the heavens more gorgeous, sparkling favour and disdain, courteous and yet coy, as if in them Venus had placed all her amorets, and Diana all her chastity. The trammels of her hair, folded in a caul of gold, so far surpassed the burnished glister of the metal, as the sun doth the meanest star in brightness: the tresses that folds in the brows of Apollo were not half so rich to the sight, for in her hairs it seemed love had laid herself in ambush, to entrap the proudest eye that durst gaze upon their excellence. What should I need to decipher her particular beauties, when by the censure of all she was the paragon of all earthly perfection? This Rosalynde sat, I say, with Alinda as a beholder of these sports, and made the cavaliers crack their lances with more courage: many deeds of knighthood that day were performed, and many prizes were given according to their several deserts.

At last, when the tournament ceased, the wrastling began, and the Norman presented himself as a challenger against all comers, but he looked like Hercules when he advanced himself against Achelous, so that the fury of his countenance amazed all that durst attempt to encounter with him in any deed of activity: till at last a lusty franklin of the country came with two tall men that were his sons, of good lineaments and comely personage. The eldest of these doing his obeisance to the king entered the list, and presented himself to the Norman, who straight coped with him, and as a man that would triumph in the glory of his strength,

c

roused himself with such fury, that not only he gave him
the fall, but killed him with the weight of his corpulent
personage: which the younger brother seeing, leaped presently
into the place, and thirsty after the revenge, assailed the
Norman with such valour, that at the first encounter he
brought him to his knees; which repulsed so the Norman,
that, recovering himself, fear of disgrace doubling his
strength, he stepped so sternly to the young franklin, that
taking him up in his arms he threw him against the ground
so violently, that he broke his neck, and so ended his
days with his brother.   At this unlooked for massacre
the people murmured, and were all in a deep passion of
pity; but the franklin, father unto these, never changed
his countenance, but as a man of a courageous resolution
took up the bodies of his sons without show of outward
discontent.

All this while stood Rosader and saw this tragedy; who,
noting the undoubted virtue of the franklin's mind, alighted
off from his horse, and presently sate down on the grass,
and commanded his boy to pull off his boots, making him
ready to try the strength of this champion.   Being furnished
as he would, he clapped the franklin on the shoulder and said
thus:

' Bold yeoman, whose sons have ended the term of their
years with honour, for that I see thou scornest fortune
with patience, and thwartest the injury of fate with content
in brooking the death of thy sons, stand awhile, and either

see me make a third in their tragedy, or else revenge their fall with an honourable triumph.'

The franklin, seeing so goodly a gentleman to give him such courteous comfort, gave him hearty thanks, with promise to pray for his happy success. With that Rosader vailed bonnet to the king, and lightly leaped within the lists, where noting more the company than the combatant, he cast his eye upon the troop of ladies that glistered there like the stars of heaven ; but at last, Love, willing to make him as amorous as he was valiant, presented him with the sight of Rosalynde, whose admirable beauty so inveigled the eye of Rosader, that forgetting himself, he stood and fed his looks on the favour of Rosalynde's face ; which she perceiving blushed, which was such a doubling of her beauteous excellence, that the bashful red of Aurora at the sight of unacquainted Phaeton, was not half so glorious.

The Norman seeing this young gentleman fettered in the looks of the ladies drave him out of his *memento* with a shake by the shoulder. Rosader looking back with an angry frown, as if he had been wakened from some pleasant dream, discovered to all by the fury of his countenance that he was a man of some high thoughts : but when they all noted his youth and the sweetness of his visage, with a general applause of favours, they grieved that so goodly a young man should venture in so base an action ; but seeing it were to his dishonour to hinder him from his enterprise, they wished him to be graced with the palm of victory.

After Rosader was thus called out of his *memento* by the Norman, he roughly clapped to him with so fierce an encounter, that they both fell to the ground, and with the violence of the fall were forced to breathe ; in which space the Norman called to mind by all tokens, that this was he whom Saladyne had appointed him to kill ; which conjecture made him stretch every limb, and try every sinew, that working his death he might recover the gold which so bountifully was promised him.   On the contrary part, Rosader while he breathed was not idle, but still cast his eye upon Rosalynde, who to encourage him with a favour, lent him such an amorous look, as might have made the most coward desperate : which glance of Rosalynde so fired the passionate desires of Rosader, that turning to the Norman he ran upon him and braved him with a strong encounter.   The Norman received him as valiantly, that there was a sore combat, hard to judge on whose side fortune would be prodigal.   At last Rosader, calling to mind the beauty of his new mistress, the fame of his father's honours, and the disgrace that should fall to his house by his misfortune, roused himself and threw the Norman against the ground, falling upon his chest with so willing a weight, that the Norman yielded nature her due, and Rosader the victory.

The death of this champion, as it highly contented the franklin, as a man satisfied with revenge, so it drew the king and all the peers into a great admiration, that so young years and so beautiful a personage should contain such martial excellence; but when they knew him to be the youngest son of Sir John of Bordeaux, the king rose from his seat and embraced him, and the peers entreated him with all favourable courtesy, commending both his valour and his virtues, wishing him to go forward in such haughty deeds, that he might attain to the glory of his father's honourable fortunes.

As the king and lords graced him with embracing, so the ladies favoured him with their looks, especially Rosalynde, whom the beauty and valour of Rosader had already touched : but she accounted love a toy, and fancy a momentary passion, that as it was taken in with a gaze, might be shaken off with a wink, and therefore feared not to dally in the flame ; and to make Rosader know she affected him, took from her neck a jewel, and sent it by a page to the young gentleman. The prize that Venus gave to Paris was not half so pleasing to the Troyan as this gem was to Rosader ; for if fortune had sworn to make him sole monarch of the world, he would rather have refused such dignity, than have lost the jewel sent him by Rosalynde. To return her with the like he was unfurnished, and yet that he might more than in his looks discover his affection, he stepped into a tent, and taking pen and paper wrote this fancy :

> Two suns at once from one fair heaven there shined,
>   Ten branches from two boughs, tipped all with roses,
> Pure locks more golden than is gold refined,
>   Two pearled rows that nature's pride encloses ;

> Two mounts fair marble-white, down-soft and dainty,
>   A snow-dyed orb, where love increased by pleasure
> Full woeful makes my heart, and body fainty:
>   Her fair, my woe, exceeds all thought and measure.
> In lines confused my luckless harm appeareth,
>   Whom sorrow clouds, whom pleasant smiling cleareth.

This sonnet he sent to Rosalynde, which when she read she
blushed, but with a sweet content in that she perceived love
had allotted her so amorous a servant.

Leaving her to her new entertained fancies, again to Rosader,
who triumphing in the glory of this conquest, accompanied
with a troop of young gentlemen that were desirous to be his
familiars, went home to his brother Saladyne's, who was
walking before the gates, to hear what success his brother
Rosader should have, assuring himself of his death, and
devising how with dissimuled sorrow to celebrate his funerals.
As he was in his thought, he cast up his eye, and saw where
Rosader returned with the garland on his head, as having
won the prize, accompanied with a crew of boon companions.
Grieved at this, he stepped in and shut the gate. Rosader
seeing this, and not looking for such unkind entertainment,
blushed at the disgrace, and yet smothering his grief with a
smile, he turned to the gentlemen, and desired them to hold
his brother excused, for he did not this upon any malicious
intent or niggardize, but being brought up in the country,
he absented himself as not finding his nature fit for such
youthful company. Thus he sought to shadow abuses
proffered him by his brother, but in vain, for he could by

no means be suffered to enter: whereupon he ran his foot
against the door, and broke it open, drawing his sword, and
entering boldly into the hall, where he found none, for all
were fled, but one Adam Spencer, an Englishman, who had
been an old and trusty servant to Sir John of Bordeaux.
He for the love he bare to his deceased master, favoured
the part of Rosader, and gave him and his such entertainment
as he could.   Rosader gave him thanks, and looking about,
seeing the hall empty, said:

'Gentlemen, you are welcome; frolic and be merry: you
shall be sure to have wine enough, whatsoever your fare
be.   I tell you, cavaliers, my brother hath in his house five
tun of wine, and as long as that lasteth, I beshrew him that
spares his liquor.'

With that he burst open the buttery door, and with the
help of Adam Spencer covered the tables, and set down whatsoever he could find in the house; but what they wanted in
meat, Rosader supplied with drink, yet had they royal cheer,
and withal such hearty welcome as would have made the
coarsest meats seem delicates.   After they had feasted and
frolicked it twice or thrice with an upsee freeze, they all took
their leaves of Rosader and departed.   As soon as they were
gone, Rosader growing impatient of the abuse, drew his
sword, and swore to be revenged on the discourteous Saladyne;
yet by the means of Adam Spencer, who sought to continue
friendship and amity betwixt the brethren, and through
the flattering submission of Saladyne, they were once again

reconciled, and put up all forepassed injuries with a peaceable
agreement, living together for a good space in such brotherly
love, as did not only rejoice the servants, but made all the
gentlemen and bordering neighbours glad of such friendly
concord.   Saladyne, hiding fire in the straw, and concealing
a poisoned hate in a peaceable countenance, yet deferring the
intent of his wrath till fitter oportunity, he showed himself
a great favourer of his brother's virtuous endeavours : where
leaving them in this happy league, let us return to Rosalynde.

Rosalynde returning home from the triumph, after she
waxed solitary love presented her with the idea of Rosader's
perfection, and taking her at discovert struck her so deep,
as she felt herself grow passing passionate.   She began to
call to mind the comeliness of his person, the honour of his
parents, and the virtues that, excelling both, made him so
gracious in the eyes of every one.   Sucking in thus the honey
of love by imprinting in her thoughts his rare qualities, she
began to surfeit with the contemplation of his virtuous conditions ; but when she called to remembrance her present estate,
and the hardness of her fortunes, desire began to shrink,
and fancy to vail bonnet, that between a Chaos of confused
thoughts she began to debate with herself in this manner :

'Infortunate Rosalynde, whose misfortunes are more than
thy years, and whose passions are greater than thy patience !
Rosalynde's   The blossoms of thy youth are mixed with the
passion.   frosts of envy, and the hope of thy ensuing
fruits perish in the bud.   Thy father is by Torismond

banished from the crown, and thou, the unhappy daughter of a king, detained captive, living as disquieted in thy thoughts as thy father discontented in his exile. Ah Rosalynde, what cares wait upon a crown! what griefs are incident to dignity! what sorrows haunt royal palaces! The greatest seas have the sorest storms, the highest birth subject to the most bale, and of all trees the cedars soonest shake with the wind: small currents are ever calm, low valleys not scorched in any lightnings, nor base men tied to any baleful prejudice. Fortune flies, and if she touch poverty it is with her heel, rather disdaining their want with a frown, than envying their wealth with disparagement. O Rosalynde, hadst thou been born low, thou hadst not fallen so high, and yet being great of blood thine honour is more, if thou brookest misfortune with patience. Suppose I contrary fortune with content, yet fates unwilling to have me anyway happy, have forced love to set my thoughts on fire with fancy. Love, Rosalynde! becometh it women in distress to think of love? Tush, desire hath no respect of persons: Cupid is blind and shooteth at random, as soon hitting a rag as a robe, and piercing as soon the bosom of a captive as the breast of a libertine. Thou speakest it, poor Rosalynde, by experience; for being every way distressed, surcharged with cares, and overgrown with sorrows, yet amidst the heap of all these mishaps, love hath lodged in thy heart the perfection of young Rosader, a man every way absolute as well for his inward life, as for his outward lineaments, able to content the eye

Oneonta Public Library

with beauty, and the ear with the report of his virtue.   But
consider, Rosalynde, his fortunes, and thy present estate :
thou art poor and without patrimony, and yet the daughter
of a prince ; he a younger brother, and void of such possessions as either might maintain thy dignities or revenge thy
father's injuries.   And hast thou not learned this of other
ladies, that lovers cannot live by looks, that women's ears are
sooner content with a dram of *give me* than a pound of *hear
me,* that gold is sweeter than eloquence, that love is a fire
and wealth is the fuel, that Venus' coffers should be ever
full ? Then, Rosalynde, seeing Rosader is poor, think him
less beautiful because he is in want, and account his
virtues but qualities of course for that he is not endued
with wealth.   Doth not Horace tell thee what method is
to be used in love ?

> Quaerenda pecunia primum, post nummos virtus.

Tush, Rosalynde, be not over rash : leap not before thou
look : either love such a one as may with his lands purchase
thy liberty, or else love not at all.   Choose not a fair face
with an empty purse, but say as most women use to say :

> Si nihil attuleris, ibis Homere foras.

Why, Rosalynde ! can such base thoughts harbour in such
high beauties ? can the degree of a princess, the daughter of
Gerismond harbour such servile conceits, as to prize gold
more than honour, or to measure a gentleman by his wealth,

not by his virtues? No, Rosalynde, blush at thy base resolution, and say, if thou lovest, either Rosader or none.   And
why? because Rosader is both beautiful and virtuous.'
Smiling to herself to think of her new-entertained passions,
taking up her lute that lay by her, she warbled out this ditty :

ROSALYNDE'S MADRIGAL

Love in my bosom like a bee
    Doth suck his sweet :
Now with his wings he plays with me,
    Now with his feet.
Within mine eyes he makes his nest,
His bed amidst my tender breast ;
My kisses are his daily feast,
And yet he robs me of my rest.
    Ah, wanton, will ye ?

And if I sleep, then percheth he
    With pretty flight,
And makes his pillow of my knee
    The livelong night.
Strike I my lute, he tunes the string,
He music plays if so I sing ;
He lends me every lovely thing,
Yet cruel he my heart doth sting.
    Whist, wanton, still ye !

Else I with roses every day
    Will whip you hence,
And bind you, when you long to play,
    For your offence ;

I'll shut mine eyes to keep you in,
I'll make you fast it for your sin,
I'll count your power not worth a pin.
Alas, what hereby shall I win,
　　If he gainsay me?

What if I beat the wanton boy
　　With many a rod?
He will repay me with annoy,
　　Because a God.
Then sit thou safely on my knee,
And let thy bower my bosom be;
Lurk in mine eyes, I like of thee.
O Cupid, so thou pity me,
　　Spare not but play thee.

Scarce had Rosalynde ended her madrigal, before Torismond came in with his daughter Alinda and many of the
peers of France, who were enamoured of her beauty; which
Torismond perceiving, fearing lest her perfection might be
the beginning of his prejudice, and the hope of his fruit end
in the beginning of her blossoms, he thought to banish her
from the court: 'for,' quoth he to himself, 'her face is so full
of favour, that it pleads pity in the eye of every man; her
beauty is so heavenly and divine, that she will prove to me
as Helen did to Priam; some one of the peers will aim
at her love, end the marriage, and then in his wife's right
attempt the kingdom. To prevent therefore *had I wist* in
all these actions, she tarries not about the court, but shall,
as an exile, either wander to her father, or else seek other

fortunes.' In this humour, with a stern countenance full of wrath, he breathed out this censure unto her before the peers, that charged her that that night she were not seen about the court: 'for,' quoth he, ' I have heard of thy aspiring speeches, and intended treasons.' This doom was strange unto Rosalynde, and presently, covered with the shield of her innocence, she boldly brake out in reverent terms to have cleared herself; but Torismond would admit of no reason, nor durst his lords plead for Rosalynde, although her beauty had made some of them passionate, seeing the figure of wrath portrayed in his brow. Standing thus all mute, and Rosalynde amazed, Alinda, who loved her more than herself, with grief in her heart and tears in her eyes, falling down on her knees, began to entreat her father thus :

' If, mighty Torismond, I offend in pleading for my friend, let the law of amity crave pardon for my boldness; for where there is depth of affection, there friendship alloweth a privilege. Rosalynde and I *Alinda's oration to her father* have been fostered up from our infancies, *in defence of* and nursed under the harbour of our con- *fair Rosalynde.* versing together with such private familiarities, that custom had wrought a union of our nature, and the sympathy of our affections such a secret love, that we have two bodies and one soul. Then marvel not, great Torismond, if, seeing my friend distressed, I find myself perplexed with a thousand sorrows; for her virtuous and honourable thoughts, which are the glories that maketh women excellent, they be such as may challenge love, and rase out suspicion. Her obedience to your majesty I refer to the censure of your own eye, that since her father's exile had smothered all griefs with patience, and in the absence of nature, hath honoured you with all duty, as her own father by nouriture, not in word uttering any discontent, nor in thought, as far as conjecture may reach, hammering on revenge ; only in all her actions seeking to please you, and to win my favour. Her wisdom, silence, chastity, and other such rich qualities, I need not decipher ; only it rests for me to conclude in one word, that she is innocent. If then, fortune, who triumphs in a variety of miseries, hath presented some envious person, as minister of her intended stratagem, to taint Rosalynde with any surmise of treason, let him be brought to her face, and confirm his accusation by witnesses ; which proved, let her die, and Alinda will execute the massacre. If none can avouch any confirmed relation of her intent, use justice, my lord, it is the glory of a king, and let her live in your wonted favour ; for if you banish her, myself, as copartner of her hard fortunes, will participate in exile some part of her extremities.'

Torismond, at this speech of Alinda, covered his face with such a frown, as tyranny seemed to sit triumphant in his forehead, and checked her up with such taunts, as made the lords, that only were hearers, to tremble.

'Proud girl,' quoth he, 'hath my looks made thee so light of tongue, or my favours encouraged thee to be so forward, that thou darest presume to preach after thy father ?

Hath not my years more experience than thy youth, and the winter of mine age deeper insight into civil policy, than the prime of thy flourishing days ? The old lion avoids the toils, where the young one leaps into the net: the care of age is provident and foresees much : suspicion is a virtue, where a man holds his enemy in his bosom. Thou, fond girl, measurest all by present affection, and as thy heart loves, thy thoughts censure ; but if thou knowest that in liking Rosalynde thou hatchest up a bird to peck out thine own eyes, thou wouldst entreat as much for her absence as now thou delightest in her presence. But why do I allege policy to thee ? Sit you down, housewife, and fall to your needle : if idleness make you so wanton, or liberty so malapert, I can quickly tie you to a sharper task. And you, maid, this night be packing, either into Arden to your father, or whither best it shall content your humour, but in the court you shall not abide.'

This rigorous reply of Torismond nothing amazed Alinda, for still she prosecuted her plea in the defence of Rosalynde, wishing her father, if his censure might not be reversed, that he would appoint her partner of her exile ; which if he refused to do, either she would by some secret means steal out and follow her, or else end her days with some desperate kind of death. When Torismond heard his daughter so resolute, his heart was so hardened against her, that he set down a definite and peremptory sentence, that they should both be banished, which presently was done, the tyrant rather choosing to hazard the loss of his only child than anyways to put in question the state of his kingdom; so suspicious and fearful is the conscience of an usurper. Well, although his lords persuaded him to retain his own daughter, yet his resolution might not be reversed, but both of them must away from the court without either more company or delay. In he went with great melancholy, and left these two ladies alone. Rosalynde waxed very sad, and sate down and wept. Alinda she smiled, and sitting by her friend began thus to comfort her:

'Why, how now, Rosalynde, dismayed with a frown of contrary fortune? Have I not oft heard thee say, that high minds were discovered in fortune's con- *Alinda's* tempt, and heroical scene in the depth of *comfort to* extremities? Thou wert wont to tell others *perplexed* that complained of distress, that the sweetest *Rosalynde.* salve for misery was patience, and the only medicine for want that precious implaister of content. Being such a good physician to others, wilt thou not minister receipts to thyself? But perchance thou wilt say:

Consulenti nunquam caput doluit.

Why then, if the patients that are sick of this disease can find in themselves neither reason to persuade, nor art to cure, yet, Rosalynde, admit of the counsel of a friend, and apply the salves that may appease thy passions. If thou grievest that being the daughter of a prince, and envy thwarteth thee with such hard exigents, think that royalty is a fair mark, that crowns have crosses when mirth is in cottages; that the fairer the rose is, the sooner it is bitten with caterpillars; the more orient the pearl is, the more apt to take a blemish; and the greatest birth, as it hath most honour, so it hath much envy. If then fortune aimeth at the fairest, be patient Rosalynde, for first by thine exile thou goest to thy father: nature is higher prized than wealth, and the love of one's parents ought to be more precious than all dignities. Why then doth my Rosalynde grieve at the frown of Torismond, who by offering her a prejudice proffers her a greater pleasure? and more, mad lass, to be melancholy, when thou hast with thee Alinda, a friend who will be a faithful copartner of all thy misfortunes, who hath left her father to follow thee, and chooseth rather to brook all extremities than to forsake thy presence. What, Rosalynde,

Solamen miseris socios habuisse doloris.

Cheerly, woman: as we have been bed-fellows in royalty, we will be fellow-mates in poverty: I will ever be thy Alinda, and thou shalt ever rest to me Rosalynde; so shall the world canonize our friendship, and speak of Rosalynde and Alinda, as they did of Pylades and Orestes. And if ever fortune smile, and we return to our former honour, then folding ourselves in the sweet of our friendship, we shall merrily say, calling to mind our forepassed miseries:

Olim haec meminisse juvabit.'

D

At this Rosalynde began to comfort her, and after she had wept a few kind tears in the bosom of her Alinda, she gave her hearty thanks, and then they sat them down to consult how they should travel. Alinda grieved at nothing but that they might have no man in their company, saying it would be their greatest prejudice in that two women went wandering without either guide or attendant.

'Tush,' quoth Rosalynde, 'art thou a woman, and hast not a sudden shift to prevent a misfortune? I, thou seest, am of a tall stature, and would very well become the person and apparel of a page; thou shalt be my mistress, and I will play the man so properly, that, trust me, in what company soever I come I will not be discovered. I will buy me a suit, and have my rapier very handsomely at my side, and if any knave offer wrong, your page will show him the point of his weapon.'

At this Alinda smiled, and upon this they agreed, and presently gathered up all their jewels, which they trussed up in a casket, and Rosalynde in all haste provided her of robes, and Alinda, from her royal weeds, put herself in more home-like attire. Thus fitted to the purpose, away go these two friends, having now changed their names, Alinda being called Aliena, and Rosalynde Ganymede. They travelled along the vineyards, and by many by-ways at last got to the forest side, where they travelled by the space of two or three days without seeing any creature, being often in danger of wild beasts, and pained with many passionate sorrows. Now the black ox began to tread on their feet, and Alinda thought of her wonted royalty; but when she cast her eyes on her Rosalynde, she thought every danger a step to honour. Passing thus on along, about midday they came to a fountain, compassed with a grove of cypress trees, so cunningly and curiously planted, as if some goddess had entreated nature in that place to make her an arbour. By this fountain sat Aliena and her Ganymede, and forth they pulled such victuals as they had, and fed as merrily as if they had been in Paris with all the king's delicates, Aliena only grieving that they could not so much as meet with a shepherd to discourse them the way to some place where they might make their abode. At last Ganymede casting up his eye espied where on a tree was engraven certain verses; which as soon as he espied, he cried out :

'Be of good cheer, mistress, I spy the figures of men ; for here in these trees be engraven certain verses of shepherds, or some other swains that inhabit hereabout.'

With that Aliena start up joyful to hear these news, and looked, where they found carved in the bark of a pine tree this passion :

Montanus's Passion

Hadst thou been born whereas perpetual cold
Makes Tanais hard, and mountains silver old ;
Had I complained unto a marble stone,
Or to the floods bewrayed my bitter moan,
　I then could bear the burthen of my grief;

But even the pride of countries at thy birth,
Whilst heavens did smile, did new array the earth
                    With flowers chief;
Yet thou, the flower of beauty blessèd born,
Hast pretty looks, but all attired in scorn.
Had I the power to weep sweet Mirrha's tears,
Or by my plaints to pierce repining ears;
Hadst thou the heart to smile at my complaint,
To scorn the woes that doth my heart attaint,
    I then could bear the burthen of my grief:
But not my tears, but truth with thee prevails,
And seeming sour my sorrows thee assails:
                    Yet small relief;
For if thou wilt thou art of marble hard,
And if thou please my suit shall soon be heard.

'No doubt,' quoth Aliena, 'this poesy is the passion of some perplexed shepherd, that being enamoured of some fair and beautiful shepherdess, suffered some sharp repulse, and therefore complained of the cruelty of his mistress.'

'You may see,' quoth Ganymede, 'what mad cattle you women be, whose hearts sometimes are made of adamant that will touch with no impression, and sometime of wax that is fit for every form: they delight to be courted, and then they glory to seem coy, and when they are most desired then they freeze with disdain: and this fault is so common to the sex, that you see it painted out in the shepherd's passions, who found his mistress as froward as he was enamoured.'

'And I pray you,' quoth Aliena, 'if your robes were off, what mettle are you made of that you are so satirical against women ? Is it not a foul bird defiles the own nest ? Beware, Ganymede, that Rosader hear you not, if he do, perchance you will make him leap so far from love, that he will anger every vein in your heart.'

'Thus,' quoth Ganymede, 'I keep decorum : I speak now as I am Aliena's page, not as I am Gerismond's daughter ; for put me but into a petticoat, and I will stand in defiance to the uttermost, that women are courteous, constant, virtuous, and what not.'

'Stay there,' quoth Aliena, 'and no more words, for yonder be characters graven upon the bark of the tall beech tree.'

'Let us see,' quoth Ganymede ; and with that they read a fancy written to this effect :

> First shall the heavens want starry light,
>   The seas be robbèd of their waves,
> The day want sun, and sun want bright,
>   The night want shade, the dead men graves,
> The April flowers and leaf and tree,
> Before I false my faith to thee.
>
> First shall the tops of highest hills
>   By humble plains be overpried,
> And poets scorn the Muses' quills,
>   And fish forsake the water glide,
> And Iris loose her coloured weed,
> Before I fail thee at thy need.

First direful hate shall turn to peace,
　And love relent in deep disdain,
And death his fatal stroke shall cease,
　And envy pity every pain,
And pleasure mourn and sorrow smile,
Before I talk of any guile.

First time shall stay his stayless race,
　And winter bless his brows with corn,
And snow bemoisten July's face,
　And winter spring, and summer mourn,
Before my pen, by help of fame,
Cease to recite thy sacred name.

MONTANUS.

'No doubt,' quoth Ganymede, 'this protestation grew from one full of passions.'

'I am of that mind too,' quoth Aliena, 'but see, I pray, when poor women seek to keep themselves chaste, how men woo them with many feigned promises; alluring with sweet words as the Sirens, and after proving as trothless as Aeneas. Thus promised Demophoon to his Phyllis, but who at last grew more false?'

'The reason was,' quoth Ganymede, 'that they were women's sons, and took that fault of their mother, for if man had grown from man, as Adam did from the earth, men had never been troubled with inconstancy.'

'Leave off,' quoth Aliena, 'to taunt thus bitterly, or else I'll pull off your page's apparel, and whip you, as Venus doth her wantons, with nettles.'

' So you will,' quoth Ganymede, ' persuade me to flattery, and that needs not: but come, seeing we have found here by this fount the tract of shepherds by their madrigals and roundelays, let us forward ; for either we shall find some folds, sheepcotes, or else some cottages wherein for a day or two to rest.'

'Content,' quoth Aliena, and with that they rose up, and marched forward till towards the even, and then coming into a fair valley, compassed with mountains, whereon grew many pleasant shrubs, they might descry where two flocks of sheep did feed. Then, looking about, they might perceive where an old shepherd sat, and with him a young swaine, under a covert most pleasantly situated. The ground where they sat was diapered with Flora's riches, as if she meant to wrap Tellus in the glory of her vestments : round about in the form of an amphitheatre were most curiously planted pine trees, interseamed with limons and citrons, which with the thickness of their boughs so shadowed the place, that Phoebus could not pry into the secret of that arbour ; so united were the tops with so thick a closure, that Venus might there in her jollity have dallied unseen with her dearest paramour. Fast by, to make the place more gorgeous, was there a fount so crystalline and clear, that it seemed Diana with her Dryades and Hamadryades had that spring, as the secret of all their bathings. In this glorious arbour sat these two shepherds, seeing their sheep feed, playing on their pipes many pleasant tunes, and from music

and melody falling into much amorous chat.   Drawing more
nigh we might descry the countenance of the one to be full
of sorrow, his face to be the very portraiture of discontent,
and his eyes full of woes, that living he seemed to die : we,
to hear what these were, stole privily behind the thicket,
where we overheard this discourse :

A PLEASANT ECLOGUE BETWEEN MONTANUS AND CORYDON

Corydon

Say, shepherd's boy, what makes thee greet so sore ?
Why leaves thy pipe his pleasure and delight ?
Young are thy years, thy cheeks with roses dight :
Then sing for joy, sweet swain, and sigh no more.

This milk-white poppy, and this climbing pine
Both promise shade ; then sit thee down and sing,
And make these woods with pleasant notes to ring,
Till Phoebus deign all westward to decline.

Montanus

Ah, Corydon, unmeet is melody
To him whom proud contempt hath overborne :
Slain are my joys by Phoebe's bitter scorn ;
Far hence my weal, and near my jeopardy.

Love's burning brand is couchèd in my breast,
Making a Phoenix of my faintful heart :
And though his fury do enforce my smart,
Ay blithe am I to honour his behest.

Prepared to woes, since so my Phoebe wills,
My looks dismayed, since Phoebe will disdain ;
I banish bliss and welcome home my pain :
So stream my tears as showers from Alpine hills.

In error's mask I blindfold judgment's eye,
I fetter reason in the snares of lust,
I seem secure, yet know not how to trust ;
I live by that which makes me living die.

Devoid of rest, companion of distress,
Plague to myself, consumèd by my thought,
How may my voice or pipe in tune be brought,
Since I am reft of solace and delight ?

Corydon

Ah, lorrel lad, what makes thee hery love ?
A sugared harm, a poison full of pleasure,
A painted shrine full filled with rotten treasure ;
A heaven in show, a hell to them that prove.

A gain in seeming, shadowed still with want,
A broken staff which folly doth uphold,
A flower that fades with every frosty cold,
An orient rose sprung from a withered plant.

A minute's joy to gain a world of grief,
A subtle net to snare the idle mind,
A seeing scorpion, yet in seeming blind,
A poor rejoice, a plague without relief.

Forthy, Montanus, follow mine arede,
Whom age hath taught the trains that fancy useth,
Leave foolish love, for beauty wit abuseth,
And drowns, by folly, virtue's springing seed

Montanus

So blames the child the flame because it burns,
And bird the snare because it doth entrap,
And fools true love because of sorry hap,
And sailors curse the ship that overturns.

But would the child forbear to play with flame,
And birds beware to trust the fowler's gin,
And fools foresee before they fall and sin,
And masters guide their ships in better frame ;

The child would praise the fire because it warms,
And birds rejoice to see the fowler fail,
And fools prevent before their plagues prevail,
And sailors bless the barque that saves from harms

Ah, Corydon, though many be thy years,
And crooked elde hath some experience left,
Yet is thy mind of judgment quite bereft,
In view of love, whose power in me appears.

The ploughman little wots to turn the pen,
Or bookman skills to guide the ploughman's cart
Nor can the cobbler count the terms of art,
Nor base men judge the thoughts of mighty men

Nor withered age, unmeet for beauty's guide,
Uncapable of love's impression,
Discourse of that whose choice possession
May never to so base a man be tied.

But I, whom nature makes of tender mould,
And youth most pliant yields to fancy's fire,
Do build my haven and heaven on sweet desire
On sweet desire, more dear to me than gold.

Think I of love, oh, how my lines aspire!
How haste the Muses to embrace my brows,
And hem my temples in with laurel boughs,
And fill my brains with chaste and holy fire!

Then leave my lines their homely equipage,
Mounted beyond the circle of the sun:
Amazed I read the stile when I have done,
And hery love that sent that heavenly rage.

Of Phoebe then, of Phoebe then I sing,
Drawing the purity of all the spheres,
The pride of earth, or what in heaven appears,
Her honoured face and fame to light to bring.

In fluent numbers, and in pleasant veins,
I rob both sea and earth of all their state,
To praise her parts: I charm both time and fate,
To bless the nymph that yields me lovesick pains.

My sheep are turned to thoughts, whom froward will
Guides in the restless labyrinth of love;
Fear lends them pasture wheresoe'er they move,
And by their death their life reneweth still.

My sheephook is my pen, mine oaten reed
My paper, where my many woes are written.
Thus silly swain, with love and fancy bitten,
I trace the plains of pain in woeful weed.

Yet are my cares, my broken sleeps, my tears,
My dreams, my doubts, for Phoebe sweet to me:
Who waiteth heaven in sorrow's vale must be,
And glory shines where danger most appears.

Then, Corydon, although I blithe me not,
Blame me not, man, since sorrow is my sweet:
So willeth love, and Phoebe thinks it meet,
And kind Montanus liketh well his lot.

Corydon

O stayless youth, by error so misguided,
Where will proscribeth laws to perfect wits,
Where reason mourns, and blame in triumph sits,
And folly poisoneth all that time provided !

With wilful blindness bleared, prepared to shame,
Prone to neglect Occasion when she smiles :
Alas, that love, by fond and froward guiles,
Should make thee tract the path to endless blame !

Ah, my Montanus, cursèd is the charm,
That hath bewitchèd so thy youthful eyes.
Leave off in time to like these vanities,
Be forward to thy good, and fly thy harm.

As many bees as Hybla daily shields,
As many fry as fleet on ocean's face,
As many herds as on the earth do trace,
As many flowers as deck the fragrant fields,

As many stars as glorious heaven contains,
As many storms as wayward winter weeps,
As many plagues as hell enclosèd keeps,
So many griefs in love, so many pains.

Suspicions, thoughts, desires, opinions, prayers,
Mislikes, misdeeds, fond joys, and feignèd peace,
Illusions, dreams, great pains, and small increase,
Vows, hopes, acceptance, scorns, and deep despairs,

Truce, war, and woe do wait at beauty's gate;
Time lost, laments, reports, and privy grudge,
And last, fierce love is but a partial judge,
Who yields for service shame, for friendship hate.

Montanus

All adder-like I stop mine ears, fond swain,
So charm no more, for I will never change.
Call home thy flocks in time that straggling range,
For lo, the sun declineth hence amain.

Terentius

In amore haec omnia insunt vitia : induciae, inimicitiae, bellum,
pax rursum : incerta haec si tu postules ratione certa fieri, nihilo
plus agas, quam si des operam, ut cum ratione insanias.

The shepherds having thus ended their eclogue, Aliena
stepped with Ganymede from behind the thicket ; at whose
sudden sight the shepherds arose, and Aliena saluted them
thus :

'Shepherds, all hail, for such we deem you by your
flocks, and lovers, good luck, for such you seem by your
passions, our eyes being witness of the one, and our ears
of the other. Although not by love, yet by fortune, I
am a distressed gentlewoman, as sorrowful as you are
passionate, and as full of woes as you of perplexed thoughts.
Wandering this way in a forest unknown, only I and my
page, wearied with travel, would fain have some place of
rest. May you appoint us any place of quiet harbour, be it
never so mean, I shall be thankful to you, contented in
myself, and grateful to whosoever shall be mine host.'

Corydon, hearing the gentlewoman speak so courteously, returned her mildly and reverently this answer:

'Fair mistress, we return you as hearty a welcome as you gave us a courteous salute. A shepherd I am, and this a lover, as watchful to please his wench as to feed his sheep: full of fancies, and therefore, say I, full of follies. Exhort him I may, but persuade him I cannot; for love admits neither of counsel nor reason. But leaving him to his passions, if you be distressed, I am sorrowful such a fair creature is crossed with calamity; pray for you I may, but relieve you I cannot. Marry, if you want lodging, if you vouch to shroud yourselves in a shepherd's cottage, my house for this night shall be your harbour.'

Aliena thanked Corydon greatly, and presently sate her down and Ganymede by her. Corydon looking earnestly upon her, and with a curious survey viewing all her perfections applauded in his thought her excellence, and pitying her distress was desirous to hear the cause of her misfortunes, began to question her thus:

'If I should not, fair damosel, occasion offence, or renew your griefs by rubbing the scar, I would fain crave so much favour as to know the cause of your misfortunes, and why, and whither you wander with your page in so dangerous a forest?'

Aliena, that was as courteous as she was fair, made this reply:

'Shepherd, a friendly demand ought never to be offensive,

and questions of courtesy carry privileged pardons in their
foreheads. Know, therefore, to discover my fortunes were
to renew my sorrows, and I should, by discoursing my mishaps, but rake fire out of the cinders. Therefore let this
suffice, gentle shepherd : my distress is as great as my
travel is dangerous, and I wander in this forest to light on
some cottage where I and my page may dwell : for I mean
to buy some farm, and a flock of sheep, and so become a
shepherdess, meaning to live low, and content me with a
country life ; for I have heard the swains say, that they
drunk without suspicion, and slept without care.'

'Marry, mistress,' quoth Corydon, 'if you mean so you came
in good time, for my landslord intends to sell both the farm
I till, and the flock I keep, and cheap you may have them
for ready money : and for a shepherd's life, O mistress, did
you but live awhile in their content, you would say the court
were rather a place of sorrow than of solace. Here, mistress, shall not fortune thwart you, but in mean misfortunes,
as the loss of a few sheep, which, as it breeds no beggary,
so it can be no extreme prejudice : the next year may
mend all with a fresh increase. Envy stirs not us, we
covet not to climb, our desires mount not above our degrees,
nor our thoughts above our fortunes. Care cannot harbour
in our cottages, nor do our homely couches know broken
slumbers : as we exceed not in diet, so we have enough to
satisfy : and, mistress, I have so much Latin, *Satis est quod
sufficit.*'

'By my troth, shepherd,' quoth Aliena, 'thou makest me in love with your country life, and therefore send for thy landslord, and I will buy thy farm and thy flocks, and thou shalt still under me be overseer of them both : only for pleasure sake I and my page will serve you, lead the flocks to the field, and fold them. Thus will I live quiet, unknown, and contented.'

This news so gladded the heart of Corydon, that he should not be put out of his farm, that putting off his shepherd's bonnet, he did her all the reverence that he might. But all this while sate Montanus in a muse, thinking of the cruelty of his Phoebe, whom he wooed long, but was in no hope to win. Ganymede, who still had the remembrance of Rosader in his thoughts, took delight to see the poor shepherd passionate, laughing at Love, that in all his actions was so imperious. At last, when she had noted his tears that stole down his cheeks, and his sighs that broke from the centre of his heart, pitying his lament, she demanded of Corydon why the young shepherd looked so sorrowful.

'O sir,' quoth he, 'the boy is in love.'

'Why,' quoth Ganymede, 'can shepherds love ? '

'Aye,' quoth Montanus, 'and overlove, else shouldst not thou see me so pensive. Love, I tell thee, is as precious in a shepherd's eye, as in the looks of a king, and we country swains entertain fancy with as great delight as the proudest courtier doth affection. Opportunity, that is the sweetest friend to Venus, harboureth in our cottages, and loyalty, the chiefest fealty that Cupid requires, is found more among shepherds than higher degrees. Then, ask not if such silly swains can love.'

'What is the cause then,' quoth Ganymede, 'that love being so sweet to thee, thou lookest so sorrowful?'

'Because,' quoth Montanus, 'the party beloved is froward, and having courtesy in her looks, holdeth disdain in her tongue's end.'

'What hath she, then,' quoth Aliena, 'in her heart?'

'Desire, I hope madam,' quoth he, 'or else, my hope lost, despair in love were death.'

As thus they chatted, the sun being ready to set, and they not having folded their sheep, Corydon requested she would sit there with her page, till Montanus and he lodged their sheep for that night.

'You shall go,' quoth Aliena, 'but first I will entreat Montanus to sing some amorous sonnet, that he made when he hath been deeply passionate.'

'That I will,' quoth Montanus, and with that he began thus :

MONTANUS'S SONNET

Phoebe sate,
Sweet she sate,
  Sweet sate Phoebe when I saw her ;
White her brow,
Coy her eye :
  Brow and eye how much you please me !

E

Words I spent,
Sighs I sent:
  Sighs and words could never draw her.
O my love,
Thou art lost,
  Since no sight could ever ease thee.

Phoebe sat
By a fount;
  Sitting by a fount I spied her:
Sweet her touch,
Rare her voice:
  Touch and voice what may distain you?
As she sung
I did sigh,
  And by sighs whilst that I tried her,
O mine eyes!
You did lose
  Her first sight whose want did pain you.

Phoebe's flocks,
White as wool:
  Yet were Phoebe's locks more whiter.
Phoebe's eyes
Dovelike mild:
  Dovelike eyes, both mild and cruel.
Montan swears,
In your lamps
  He will die for to delight her.
Phoebe yield,
Or I die:
  Shall true hearts be fancy's fuel?

Montanus had no sooner ended his sonnet, but Corydon
with a low courtesy rose up and went with his fellow, and
shut their sheep in the folds; and after returning to Aliena
and Ganymede, conducted them home weary to his poor
cottage.   By the way there was much good chat with Montanus about his loves, he resolving Aliena that Phoebe was
the fairest shepherdess in all France, and that in his eye her
beauty was equal with the nymphs.

' But,' quoth he, ' as of all stones the diamond is most
clearest, and yet most hard for the lapidary to cut: as of
all flowers the rose is the fairest, and yet guarded with the
sharpest prickles: so of all our country lasses Phoebe is the
brightest, but the most coy of all to stoop unto desire.   But
let her take heed,' quoth he, ' I have heard of Narcissus, who
for his high disdain against Love, perished in the folly of his
own love.'

With this they were at Corydon's cottage, where Montanus
parted from them, and they went in to rest.   Aliena and
Ganymede glad of so contented a shelter, made merry with
the poor swain; and though they had but country fare and
coarse lodging, yet their welcome was so great, and their
cares so little, that they counted their diet delicate, and
slept as soundly as if they had been in the court of Torismond.   The next morn they lay long in bed, as wearied
with the toil of unaccustomed travel; but as soon as they got
up, Aliena resolved there to set up her rest, and by the help
of Corydon swept a bargain with his landslord, and so became

mistress of the farm and the flock, herself putting on the attire of a shepherdess, and Ganymede of a young swain: every day leading forth her flocks, with such delight, that she held her exile happy, and thought no content to the bliss of a country cottage. Leaving her thus famous amongst the shepherds of Arden, again to Saladyne.

When Saladyne had a long while concealed a secret resolution of revenge, and could no longer hide fire in the flax, nor oil in the flame, for envy is like lightning, that will appear in the darkest fog, it chanced on a morning very early he called up certain of his servants, and went with them to the chamber of Rosader, which being open, he entered with his crew, and surprised his brother being asleep, and bound him in fetters, and in the midst of his hall chained him to a post. Rosader, amazed at this strange chance, began to reason with his brother about the cause of this sudden extremity, wherein he had wronged, and what fault he had committed worthy so sharp a penance. Saladyne answered him only with a look of disdain, and went his way, leaving poor Rosader in a deep perplexity; who, thus abused, fell into sundry passions, but no means of relief could be had: whereupon for anger he grew into a discontented melancholy. In which humour he continued two or three days without meat, insomuch that seeing his brother would give him no food, he fell into despair of his life. Which Adam Spencer, the old servant of Sir John of Bordeaux, seeing, touched with the duty and love he ought to his old master, felt a remorse in his conscience of his son's mishap; and therefore, although Saladyne had given a general charge to his servants that none of them upon pain of death should give either meat or drink to Rosader, yet Adam Spencer in the night rose secretly, and brought him such victuals as he could provide, and unlocked him, and set him at liberty. After Rosader had well feasted himself, and felt he was loose, straight his thoughts aimed at revenge, and now, all being asleep, he would have quit Saladyne with the method of his own mischief. But Adam Spencer did persuade him to the contrary with these reasons :

'Sir,' quoth he, 'be content, for this night go again into your old fetters, so shall you try the faith of friends, and save the life of an old servant. To-morrow hath your brother invited all your kindred and allies to a solemn breakfast, only to see you, telling them all that you are mad, and fain to be tied to a post. As soon as they come, complain to them of the abuse proffered you by Saladyne. If they redress you, why so : but if they pass over your plaints *sicco pede*, and hold with the violence of your brother before your innocence, then thus : I will leave you unlocked that you may break out at your pleasure, and at the end of the hall shall you see stand a couple of good poleaxes, one for you and another for me. When I give you a wink, shake off your chains, and let us play the men, and make havoc amongst them, drive them out of the house and maintain possession by force of arms, till the king hath made a redress of your abuses.'

These words of Adam Spencer so persuaded Rosader, that he went to the place of his punishment, and stood there while the next morning. About the time appointed, came all the guests bidden by Saladyne, whom he entreated with courteous and curious entertainment, as they all perceived their welcome to be great. The tables in the hall, where Rosader was tied, were covered, and Saladyne bringing in his guests together, showed them where his brother was bound, and was enchained as a man lunatic. Rosader made reply, and with some invectives made complaints of the wrongs proffered him by Saladyne, desiring they would in pity seek some means for his relief. But in vain, they had stopped their ears with Ulysses, that were his words never so forceable, he breathed only his passions into the wind. They, careless, sat down with Saladyne to dinner, being very frolic and pleasant, washing their heads well with wine. At last, when the fume of the grape had entered peale-meale into their brains, they began in satirical speeches to rail against Rosader: which Adam Spencer no longer brooking, gave the sign, and Rosader shaking off his chains got a poleaxe in his hand, and flew amongst them with such violence and fury, that he hurt many, slew some, and drave his brother and the rest quite out of the house. Seeing the coast clear, he shut the doors, and being sore anhungered, and seeing such good victuals, he sat him down with Adam

Spencer, and such good fellows as he knew were honest men, and there feasted themselves with such provision as Saladyne had prepared for his friends.   After they had taken their repast, Rosader rampired up the house, lest upon a sudden his brother should raise some crew of his tenants, and surprise them unawares.   But Saladyne took a contrary course, and went to the sheriff of the shire and made complaint of Rosader, who giving credit to Saladyne, in a determined resolution to revenge the gentleman's wrongs, took with him five-and-twenty tall men, and made a vow, either to break into the house and take Rosader, or else to coop him in till he made him yield by famine.   In this determination, gathering a crew together, he went forward to set Saladyne in his former estate.   News of this was brought unto Rosader, who smiling at the cowardice of his brother, brooked all the injuries of fortune with patience, expecting the coming of the sheriff.   As he walked upon the battlements of the house, he descried where Saladyne and he drew near, with a troop of lusty gallants.   At this he smiled, and called Adam Spencer, and showed him the envious treachery of his brother, and the folly of the sheriff to be so credulous.

'Now, Adam,' quoth he, 'what shall I do?   It rests for me either to yield up the house to my brother and seek a reconcilement, or else issue out, and break through the company with courage, for cooped in like a coward I will not be.   If I submit, ah Adam, I dishonour myself, and that is worse than death, for by such open disgraces, the fame of men

grows odious. If I issue out amongst them, fortune may
favour me, and I may escape with life. But suppose the
worst ; if I be slain, then my death shall be honourable to
me, and so inequal a revenge infamous to Saladyne.'

' Why then, master, forward and fear not ! Out amongst
them; they be but faint-hearted losels, and for Adam
Spencer, if he die not at your foot, say he is a dastard.'

These words cheered up so the heart of young Rosader,
that he thought himself sufficient for them all, and therefore
prepared weapons for him and Adam Spencer, and were ready
to entertain the sheriff ; for no sooner came Saladyne and
he to the gates, but Rosader, unlooked for, leaped out and
assailed them, wounded many of them, and caused the rest
to give back, so that Adam and he broke through the prease
in despite of them all, and took their way towards the
forest of Arden. This repulse so set the sheriff's heart on
fire to revenge, that he straight raised all the country, and
made hue and cry after them. But Rosader and Adam,
knowing full well the secret ways that led through the
vineyards, stole away privily through the province of Bordeaux, and escaped safe to the forest of Arden. Being
come thither, they were glad they had so good a harbour :
but fortune, who is like the chameleon, variable with every
object, and constant in nothing but inconstancy, thought
to make them mirrors of her mutability, and therefore still
crossed them thus contrarily. Thinking still to pass on by
the by-ways to get to Lyons, they chanced on a path that led

into the thick of the forest, where they wandered five or
six days without meat, that they were almost famished
finding neither shepherd nor cottage to relieve them ; and
hunger growing on so extreme, Adam Spencer, being old,
began first to faint, and sitting him down on a hill, and looking about him, espied where Rosader lay as feeble and as ill
perplexed : which sight made him shed tears, and to fall
into these bitter terms :

'Oh, how the life of man may well be compared to the
state of the ocean seas, that for every calm   *Adam Spencer's*
hath a thousand storms, resembling the rose   *speech.*
tree, that for a few fair flowers hath a multitude of sharp
prickles! All our pleasures end in pain, and our highest
delights are crossed with deepest discontents. The joys
of man, as they are few, so are they momentary, scarce ripe
before they are rotten, and withering in the blossom, either
parched with the heat of envy or fortune. Fortune, O
inconstant friend, that in all thy deeds art froward and
fickle, delighting, in the poverty of the lowest and the overthrow of the highest, to decipher thy inconstancy. Thou
standest upon a globe, and thy wings are plumed with Time's
feathers, that thou mayest ever be restless : thou art double-
faced like Janus, carrying frowns in the one to threaten,
and smiles in the other to betray : thou profferest an eel,
and performest a scorpion, and where thy greatest favours
be, there is the fear of the extremest misfortunes, so variable
are all thy actions. But why, Adam, dost thou exclaim

against Fortune? She laughs at the plaints of the distressed, and there is nothing more pleasing unto her, than to hear fools boast in her fading allurements, or sorrowful men to discover the sour of their passions. Glut her not, Adam, then with content, but thwart her with brooking all mishaps with patience. For there is no greater check to the pride of Fortune, than with a resolute courage to pass over her crosses without care. Thou art old, Adam, and thy hairs wax white: the palm tree is already full of blooms, and in the furrows of thy face appears the calendars of death. Wert thou blessed by Fortune thy years could not be many, nor the date of thy life long: then sith nature must have her due, what is it for thee to resign her debt a little before the day. Ah, it is not this which grieveth me, nor do I care what mishaps Fortune can wage against me, but the sight of Rosader that galleth unto the quick. When I remember the worships of his house, the honour of his fathers, and the virtues of himself, then do I say, that fortune and the fates are most injurious, to censure so hard extremes, against a youth of so great hope. O Rosader, thou art in the flower of thine age, and in the pride of thy years, buxom and full of May. Nature hath prodigally enriched thee with her favours, and virtue made thee the mirror of her excellence ; and now, through the decree of the unjust stars, to have all these good parts nipped in the blade, and blemished by the inconstancy of fortune ! Ah, Rosader, could I help thee, my grief were the less, and happy should my death be, if it might be the beginning of thy relief: but seeing we perish both in one extreme, it is a double sorrow. What shall I do? prevent the sight of his further misfortune with a present dispatch of mine own life? Ah, despair is a merciless sin!'

As he was ready to go forward in his passion, he looked earnestly on Rosader, and seeing him change colour, he rise up and went to him, and holding his temples, said:

'What cheer, master? though all fail, let not the heart faint: the courage of a man is showed in the resolution of his death.'

At these words Rosader lifted up his eye, and looking on Adam Spencer, began to weep.

'Ah, Adam,' quoth he, 'I sorrow not to die, but I grieve at the manner of my death. Might I with my lance encounter the enemy, and so die in the field, it were honour and content: might I, Adam, combate with some wild beast and perish as his prey, I were satisfied; but to die with hunger, O Adam, it is the extremest of all extremes!'

'Master,' quoth he, 'you see we are both in one predicament, and long I cannot live without meat; seeing therefore we can find no food, let the death of the one preserve the life of the other. I am old, and overworn with age, you are young, and are the hope of many honours: let me then die, I will presently cut my veins, and, master, with the warm blood relieve your fainting spirits: suck on that till I end, and you be comforted.'

With that Adam Spencer was ready to pull out his knife, when Rosader full of courage, though very faint, rose up, and wished Adam Spencer to sit there till his return; 'for my mind gives me,' quoth he, 'I shall bring thee meat.' With that, like a madman, he rose up, and ranged up and down the woods, seeking to encounter some wild beast with his rapier, that either he might carry his friend Adam food, or else pledge his life in pawn for his loyalty.

It chanced that day, that Gerismond, the lawful king of France banished by Torismond, who with a lusty crew of outlaws lived in that forest, that day in honour of his birth made a feast to all his bold yeomen, and frolicked it with store of wine and venison, sitting all at a long table under the shadow of limon trees. To that place by chance fortune conducted Rosader, who seeing such a crew of brave men, having store of that for want of which he and Adam perished, he stepped boldly to the board's end, and saluted the company thus :

'Whatsoever thou be that art master of these lusty squires, I salute thee as graciously as a man in extreme distress may : know that I and a fellow-friend of mine are here famished in the forest for want of food : perish we must, unless relieved by thy favours. Therefore, if thou be a gentleman, give meat to men, and to such men as are every way worthy of life. Let the proudest squire that sits at thy table rise and encounter with me in any honourable point of activity whatsoever, and if he and thou prove me not a man,

send me away comfortless.   If thou refuse this, as a niggard
of thy cates, I will have amongst you with my sword ; for
rather will I die valiantly, than perish with so cowardly an
extreme.'

Gerismond, looking him earnestly in the face, and seeing
so proper a gentleman in so bitter a passion, was moved with
so great pity, that rising from the table, he took him by the
hand and bad him welcome, willing him to sit down in his
place, and in his room not only to eat his fill, but be lord
of the feast.

'Gramercy, sir,' quoth Rosader, 'but I have a feeble
friend that lies hereby famished almost for food, aged and
therefore less able to abide the extremity of hunger than myself, and dishonour it were for me to taste one crumb, before
I made him partner of my fortunes : therefore I will run and
fetch him, and then I will gratefully accept of your proffer.'

Away hies Rosader to Adam Spencer, and tells him the
news, who was glad of so happy fortune, but so feeble he
was that he could not go ; whereupon Rosader got him up
on his back, and brought him to the place.   Which when
Gerismond and his men saw, they greatly applauded their
league of friendship ; and Rosader, having Gerismond's place
assigned him, would not sit there himself, but set down
Adam Spencer.   Well, to be short, those hungry squires fell
to their victuals, and feasted themselves with good delicates,
and great store of wine.   As soon as they had taken their
repast, Gerismond, desirous to hear what hard fortune drave

them into those bitter extremes, requested Rosader to discourse, if it were not any way prejudicial unto him, the cause of his travel. Rosader, desirous any way to satisfy the courtesy of his favourable host, first beginning his exordium with a volley of sighs, and a few lukewarm tears, prosecuted his discourse, and told him from point to point all his fortunes : how he was the youngest son of Sir John of Bordeaux, his name Rosader, how his brother sundry times had wronged him, and lastly how, for beating the sheriff and hurting his men, he fled.

'And this old man,' quoth he, 'whom I so much love and honour, is surnamed Adam Spencer, an old servant of my father's, and one, that for his love, never failed me in all my misfortunes.'

When Gerismond heard this, he fell on the neck of Rosader, and next discoursing unto him how he was Gerismond their lawful king exiled by Torismond, what familiarity had ever been betwixt his father, Sir John of Bordeaux, and him, how faithful a subject he lived, and how honourable he died, promising, for his sake, to give both him and his friend such courteous entertainment as his present estate could minister, and upon this made him one of his foresters. Rosader seeing it was the king, craved pardon for his boldness, in that he did not do him due reverence, and humbly gave him thanks for his favourable courtesy. Gerismond, not satisfied yet with news, began to inquire if he had been lately in the court of Torismond, and whether he

had seen his daughter Rosalynde or no? At this Rosader
fetched a deep sigh, and shedding many tears, could not
answer: yet at last, gathering his spirits together, he revealed
unto the king, how Rosalynde was banished, and how there
was such a sympathy of affections between Alinda and her,
that she chose rather to be partaker of her exile, than to
part fellowship; whereupon the unnatural king banished them
both: 'and now they are wandered none knows whither,
neither could any learn since their departure, the place of
their abode.' This news drave the king into a great
melancholy, that presently he arose from all the company,
and went into his privy chamber, so secret as the harbour of
the woods would allow him. The company was all dashed
at these tidings, and Rosader and Adam Spencer, having
such opportunity, went to take their rest. Where we leave
them, and return again to Torismond.

The flight of Rosader came to the ears of Torismond,
who hearing that Saladyne was sole heir of the lands of
Sir John of Bordeaux, desirous to possess such fair revenues,
found just occasion to quarrel with Saladyne about the
wrongs he proffered to his brother: and therefore, dispatching
a herehault, he sent for Saladyne in all post-haste. Who
marvelling what the matter should be, began to examine his
own conscience, wherein he had offended his highness; but
emboldened with his innocence, he boldly went with the herehault unto the court; where, as soon as he came, he was not
admitted into the presence of the king, but presently sent to

prison. This greatly amazed Saladyne, chiefly in that the
jailer had a straight charge over him, to see that he should
be close prisoner.   Many passionate thoughts came in his head,
till at last he began to fall into consideration of his former
follies, and to meditate with himself.   Leaning his head on
his hand, and his elbow on his knee, full of sorrow, grief and
disquieted passions, he resolved into these terms:

  'Unhappy Saladyne! whom folly hath led to these misfortunes, and wanton desires wrapped within the labyrinth of
Saladyne's   these calamities!   Are not the heavens doomers
complaint.   of men's deeds; and holds not God a balance
in his fist, to reward with favour, and revenge with justice?
O Saladyne, the faults of thy youth, as they were fond,
so were they foul, and not only discovering little nurture, but
blemishing the excellence of nature.   Whelps of one litter are
ever most loving, and brothers that are sons of one father
should live in friendship without jar.   O Saladyne, so it
should be; but thou hast with the deer fed against the
wind, with the crab strove against the stream, and sought
to pervert nature by unkindness.   Rosader's wrongs, the
wrongs of Rosader, Saladyne, cries for revenge; his youth
pleads to God to inflict some penance upon thee; his virtues
are pleas that enforce writs of displeasure to cross thee: thou
hast highly abused thy kind and natural brother, and the
heavens cannot spare to quite thee with punishment.   There
is no sting to the worm of conscience, no hell to a mind
touched with guilt.   Every wrong I offered him, called now to

remembrance, wringeth a drop of blood from my heart, every bad look, every frown pincheth me at the quick, and says, " Saladyne thou hast sinned against Rosader." Be penitent, and assign thyself some penance to discover thy sorrow, and pacify his wrath.'

In the depth of his passion, he was sent for to the king, who with a look that threatened death entertained him, and demanded of him where his brother was. Salaayne made answer, that upon some riot made against the sheriff of the shire, he was fled from Bordeaux, but he knew not whither.

'Nay, villain,' quoth he, 'I have heard of the wrongs thou hast proffered thy brother since the death of thy father, and by thy means have I lost a most brave and resolute chevalier. Therefore, in justice to punish thee, I spare thy life for thy father's sake, but banish thee for ever from the court and country of France; and see thy departure be within ten days, else trust me thou shalt lose thy head.'

And with that the king flew away in a rage, and left poor Saladyne greatly perplexed; who grieving at his exile, yet determined to bear it with patience, and in penance of his former follies to travel abroad in every coast till he had found out his brother Rosader. With whom now I begin.

Rosader, being thus preferred to the place of a forester by Gerismond, rooted out the remembrance of his brother's unkindness by continual exercise, traversing the groves and wild forests, partly to hear the melody of the sweet birds

F

which recorded, and partly to show his diligent endeavour
in his master's behalf. Yet whatsoever he did, or howsoever he walked, the lively image of Rosalynde remained in
memory: on her sweet perfections he fed his thoughts,
proving himself like the eagle a true-born bird, since as the
one is known by beholding the sun, so was he by regarding
excellent beauty. One day among the rest, finding a fit
opportunity and place convenient, desirous to discover his woes
to the woods, he engraved with his knife on the bark of a
myrtle tree, this pretty estimate of his mistress' perfection :

SONETTO

Of all chaste birds the Phoenix doth excell,
Of all strong beasts the lion bears the bell,
Of all sweet flowers the rose doth sweetest smell,
Of all fair maids my Rosalynde is fairest.

Of all pure metals gold is only purest,
Of all high trees the pine hath highest crest,
Of all soft sweets I like my mistress' breast,
Of all chaste thoughts my mistress' thoughts are rarest.

Of all proud birds the eagle pleaseth Jove,
Of pretty fowls kind Venus likes the dove,
Of trees Minerva doth the olive love,
Of all sweet nymphs I honour Rosalynde.

Of all her gifts her wisdom pleaseth most,
Of all her graces virtue she doth boast:
For all these gifts my life and joy is lost,
If Rosalynde prove cruel and unkind,

In these and such like passions Rosader did every day eternize the name of his Rosalynde ; and this day especially when Aliena and Ganymede, enforced by the heat of the sun to seek for shelter, by good fortune arrived in that place, where this amorous forester registered his melancholy passions. They saw the sudden change of his looks, his folded arms, his passionate sighs : they heard him often abruptly call on Rosalynde, who, poor soul, was as hotly burned as himself, but that she shrouded her pains in the cinders of honourable modesty.   Whereupon, guessing him to be in love, and according to the nature of their sex being pitiful in that behalf, they suddenly brake off his melancholy by their approach, and Ganymede shook him out of his dumps thus :

'What news, forester ? hast thou wounded some deer, and lost him in the fall?   Care not man for so small a loss : thy fees was but the skin, the shoulder, and the horns : 'tis hunter's luck to aim fair and miss; and a woodman's fortune to strike and yet go without the game.'

'Thou art beyond the mark, Ganymede,' quoth Aliena : 'his passions are greater, and his sighs discovers more loss : perhaps in traversing these thickets, he hath seen some beautiful nymph, and is grown amorous.'

'It may be so,' quoth Ganymede, 'for here he hath newly engraven some sonnet : come, and see the discourse of the forester's poems.'

Reading the sonnet over, and hearing him name Rosalynde, Aliena looked on Ganymede and laughed, and Ganymede looking back on the forester, and seeing it was Rosader, blushed ; yet thinking to shroud all under her page's apparel, she boldly returned to Rosader, and began thus :

'I pray thee tell me, forester, what is this Rosalynde for whom thou pinest away in such passions ? Is she some nymph that waits upon Diana's train, whose chastity thou hast deciphered in such epithets ? Or is she some shepherdess that haunts these plains whose beauty hath so bewitched thy fancy, whose name thou shadowest in covert under the figure of Rosalynde, as Ovid did Julia under the name of Corinna ? Or say me forsooth, is it that Rosalynde, of whom we shepherds have heard talk, she, forester, that is the daughter of Gerismond, that once was king, and now an outlaw in the forest of Arden ? '

At this Rosader fetched a deep sigh, and said :

' It is she, O gentle swain, it is she ; that saint it is whom I serve, that goddess at whose shrine I do bend all my devotions ; the most fairest of all fairs, the phoenix of all that sex, and the purity of all earthly perfection.'

'And why, gentle forester, if she be so beautiful, and thou so amorous, is there such a disagreement in thy thoughts ? Happily she resembleth the rose, that is sweet but full of prickles ? or the serpent Regius that hath scales as glorious as the sun and a breath as infectious as the Aconitum is deadly ? So thy Rosalynde may be most amiable and yet unkind ; full of favour and yet froward, coy without wit, and disdainful without reason.'

'O Shepherd,' quoth Rosader, 'knewest thou her personage, graced with the excellence of all perfection, being a harbour wherein the graces shroud their virtues, thou wouldest not breathe out such blasphemy against the beauteous Rosalynde. She is a diamond, bright but not hard, yet of most chaste operation; a pearl so orient, that it can be stained with no blemish; a rose without prickles, and a princess absolute as well in beauty as in virtue. But I, unhappy I, have let mine eye soar with the eagle against so bright a sun that I am quite blind: I have with Apollo enamoured myself of a Daphne, not, as she, disdainful, but far more chaste than Daphne: I have with Ixion laid my love on Juno, and shall, I fear, embrace nought but a cloud. Ah, Shepherd, I have reached at a star: my desires have mounted above my degree, and my thoughts above my fortunes. I being a peasant, have ventured to gaze on a princess, whose honours are too high to vouchsafe such base loves.'

'Why, forester,' quoth Ganymede, 'comfort thyself; be blithe and frolic man. Love souseth as low as she soareth high: Cupid shoots at a rag as soon as at a robe; and Venus' eye that was so curious, sparkled favour on pole-footed Vulcan. Fear not, man, women's looks are not tied to dignity's feathers, nor make they curious esteem where the stone is found, but what is the virtue. Fear not, forester; faint heart never won fair lady. But where lives Rosalynde now? at the court?'

'Oh no,' quoth Rosader, 'she lives I know not where, and

that is my sorrow; banished by Torismond, and that is my
hell : for might I but find her sacred personage, and plead
before the bar of her pity the plaint of my passions, hope tells
me she would grace me with some favour, and that would
suffice as a recompense of all my former miseries.'

'Much have I heard of thy mistress' excellence, and I know,
forester, thou canst describe her at the full, as one that hast
surveyed all her parts with a curious eye; then do me that
favour, to tell me what her perfections be.'

'That I will,' quoth Rosader, 'for I glory to make all ears
wonder at my mistress' excellence.'

And with that he pulled a paper forth his bosom, wherein
he read this :

Rosalynde's Description

Like to the clear in highest sphere
Where all imperial glory shines,
Of selfsame colour is her hair,
Whether unfolded or in twines :
    Heigh ho, fair Rosalynde.
Her eyes are sapphires set in snow,
Refining heaven by every wink :
The gods do fear whenas they glow,
And I do tremble when I think :
    Heigh ho, would she were mine.

Her cheeks are like the blushing cloud
That beautifies Aurora's face,
Or like the silver crimson shroud
That Phoebus' smiling looks doth grace :
    Heigh ho, fair Rosalynde.

Her lips are like two budded roses,
Whom ranks of lilies neighbour nigh,
Within which bounds she balm encloses,
Apt to entice a deity:
 Heigh ho, would she were mine.

Her neck, like to a stately tower
Where love himself imprisoned lies,
To watch for glances every hour
From her divine and sacred eyes:
 Heigh ho, fair Rosalynde.
Her paps are centres of delight,
Her paps are orbs of heavenly frame,
Where nature moulds the dew of light,
To feed perfection with the same:
 Heigh ho, would she were mine.

With orient pearl, with ruby red,
With marble white, with sapphire blue,
Her body every way is fed,
Yet soft in touch, and sweet in view:
 Heigh ho, fair Rosalynde.
Nature herself her shape admires,
The gods are wounded in her sight,
And Love forsakes his heavenly fires
And at her eyes his brand doth light:
 Heigh ho, would she were mine.

Then muse not, nymphs, though I bemoan
The absence of fair Rosalynde,
Since for her fair there is fairer none,
Nor for her virtues so divine:
 Heigh ho, fair Rosalynde.
 Heigh ho, my heart, would God that she were mine
   Periit, quia deperibat.

'Believe me,' quoth Ganymede, 'either the forester is an exquisite painter, or Rosalynde far above wonder; so it makes me blush to hear how women should oe so excellent, and pages so unperfect.'

Rosader beholding her earnestly, answered thus:

'Truly, gentle page, thou hast cause to complain thee wert thou the substance, but resembling the shadow content thyself; for it is excellence enough to be like the excellence of nature.'

'He hath answered you, Ganymede,' quoth Aliena, 'it is enough for pages to wait on beautiful ladies, and not to be beautiful themselves.'

'O mistress,' quoth Ganymede, 'hold you your peace, for you are partial. Who knows not, but that all women have desire to tie sovereignty to their petticoats, and ascribe beauty to themselves, where, if boys might put on their garments, perhaps they would prove as comely; if not as comely, it may be more courteous. But tell me, forester,' and with that she turned to Rosader, 'under whom maintainest thou thy walk?'

'Gentle swain, under the king of outlaws,' said he, 'the unfortunate Gerismond, who having lost his kingdom, crowneth his thoughts with content, accounting it better to govern among poor men in peace, than great men in danger.'

'But hast thou not,' said she, 'having so melancholy opportunities as this forest affordeth thee, written more sonnets in commendations of thy mistress?'

'I have, gentle swain,' quoth he, 'but they be not about me. To-morrow by dawn of day, if your flocks feed in these pastures, I will bring them you, wherein you shall read my passions whilst I feel them, judge my patience when you read it: till when I bid farewell.' So giving both Ganymede and Aliena a gentle good-night, he resorted to his lodge, leaving Aliena and Ganymede to their prittle-prattle.

'So Ganymede,' said Aliena, the forester being gone, 'you are mightily beloved; men make ditties in your praise, spend sighs for your sake, make an idol of your beauty. Believe me, it grieves me not a little to see the poor man so pensive, and you so pitiless.'

'Ah, Aliena,' quoth she, 'be not peremptory in your judgments. I hear Rosalynde praised as I am Ganymede, but were I Rosalynde, I could answer the forester: if he mourn for love, there are medicines for love: Rosalynde cannot be fair and unkind. And so, madam, you see it is time to fold our flocks, or else Corydon will frown and say you will never prove good housewife.'

With that they put their sheep into the cotes, and went home to her friend Corydon's cottage, Aliena as merry as might be that she was thus in the company of her Rosalynde; but she, poor soul, that had love her lodestar, and her thoughts set on fire with the flame of fancy, could take no rest, but being alone began to consider what passionate penance poor Rosader was enjoined to by love and fortune, that at last she fell into this humour with herself:

'Ah, Rosalynde, how the Fates have set down in their synod to make thee unhappy : for when Fortune hath done *Rosalynde passionate alone.* her worst, then Love comes in to begin a new tragedy : she seeks to lodge her son in thine eyes, and to kindle her fires in thy bosom. Beware, fond girl, he is an unruly guest to harbour ; for cutting in by entreats, he will not be thrust out by force, and her fires are fed with such fuel, as no water is able to quench. Seest thou not how Venus seeks to wrap thee in her labyrinth, wherein is pleasure at the entrance, but within, sorrows, cares, and discontent ? She is a Siren, stop thine ears to her melody ; she is a basilisk, shut thy eyes and gaze not at her lest thou perish. Thou art now placed in the country content, where are heavenly thoughts and mean desires : in those lawns where thy flocks feed Diana haunts : be as her nymphs chaste, and enemy to love, for there is no greater honour to a maid, than to account of fancy as a mortal foe to their sex. Daphne, that bonny wench, was not turned into a bay tree, as the poets feign : but for her chastity her fame was immortal, resembling the laurel that is ever green. Follow thou her steps, Rosalynde, and the rather, for that thou art an exile, and banished from the court ; whose distress, and it is appeased with patience, so it would be renewed with amorous passions. Have mind on thy forepassed fortunes ; fear the worst, and entangle not thyself with present fancies, lest loving in haste, thou repent thee at leisure. Ah, but yet, Rosalynde, it is Rosader that courts thee; one who as he is beautiful, so he is virtuous, and harboureth in his mind as many good qualities as his face is shadowed with gracious favours; and therefore, Rosalynde, stoop to love, lest, being either too coy or too cruel, Venus wax wroth, and plague thee with the reward of disdain.'

Rosalynde, thus passionate, was wakened from her dumps by Aliena, who said it was time to go to bed. Corydon swore that was true, for Charles' Wain was risen in the north. Whereupon each taking leave of other, went to their rest, all but the poor Rosalynde, who was so full of passions, that she could not possess any content. Well, leaving her to her broken slumbers, expect what was performed by them the next morning.

The sun was no sooner stepped from the bed of Aurora, but Aliena was wakened by Ganymede, who, restless all night, had tossed in her passions, saying it was then time to go to the field to unfold their sheep. Aliena, that spied where the hare was by the hounds, and could see day at a little hole, thought to be pleasant with her Ganymede, and therefore replied thus:

'What, wanton! the sun is but new up, and as yet Iris' riches lie folded in the bosom of Flora: Phoebus hath not dried up the pearled dew, and so long Corydon hath taught me, it is not fit to lead the sheep abroad, lest, the dew being unwholesome, they get the rot: but now see I the old proverb true, he is in haste whom the devil drives, and where love pricks forward, there is no worse death than delay. Ah, my good page, is there fancy in thine eye, and passions in thy heart ? What, hast thou wrapt love in thy looks, and set all thy thoughts on fire by affection ? I tell thee, it is a flame as hard to be quenched as that of Aetna. But nature must have her course : women's eyes have faculty attractive like the jet, and retentive like the diamond : they dally in the delight of fair objects, till gazing on the panther's beautiful skin, repenting experience tell them he hath a devouring paunch.'

'Come on,' quoth Ganymede, 'this sermon of yours is but a subtlety to lie still a-bed, because either you think the morning cold, or else I being gone, you would steal a nap : this shift carries no palm, and therefore up and away. And for Love, let me alone ; I'll whip him away with nettles, and set disdain as a charm to withstand his forces : and therefore look you to yourself ; be not too bold, for Venus can make you bend, nor too coy, for Cupid hath a piercing dart, that will make you cry *Peccavi.*'

'And that is it,' quoth Aliena, 'that hath raised you so early this morning.' And with that she slipped on her petticoat, and start up ; and as soon as she had made her ready, and taken her breakfast, away go these two with their bag and bottles to the field, in more pleasant content of mind than ever they were in the court of Torismond.

They came no sooner nigh the folds, but they might

see where their discontented forester was walking in his
melancholy.   As soon as Aliena saw him, she smiled and
said to Ganymede :

'Wipe your eyes, sweeting, for yonder is your sweetheart this morning in deep prayers, no doubt, to Venus,
that she may make you as pitiful as he is passionate.   Come
on, Ganymede, I pray thee, let's have a little sport with
him.'

'Content,' quoth Ganymede, and with that, to waken him
out of his deep *memento*, he began thus :

'Forester, good fortune to thy thoughts, and ease to thy
passions.   What makes you so early abroad this morn ? in
contemplation, no doubt, of your Rosalynde.   Take heed,
forester ; step not too far, the ford may be deep, and you slip
over the shoes.   I tell thee, flies have their spleen, the ants
choler, the least hairs shadows, and the smallest loves great
desires.   'Tis good, forester, to love, but not to overlove,
lest in loving her that likes not thee, thou fold thyself in
an endless labyrinth.'

Rosader, seeing the fair shepherdess and her pretty swain
in whose company he felt the greatest ease of his care, he
returned them a salute on this manner :

'Gentle shepherds, all hail, and as healthful be your
flocks as you happy in content.   Love is restless, and my
bed is but the cell of my bane, in that there I find busy
thoughts and broken slumbers : here, although everywhere

passionate, yet I brook love with more patience, in that every object feeds mine eye with variety of fancies. When I look on Flora's beauteous tapestry, checked with the pride of all her treasure, I call to mind the fair face of Rosalynde, whose heavenly hue exceeds the rose and the lily in their highest excellence : the brightness of Phoebus' shine puts me in mind to think of the sparkling flames that flew from her eyes, and set my heart first on fire : the sweet harmony of the birds, puts me in remembrance of the rare melody of her voice, which like the Siren enchanteth the ears of the hearer. Thus in contemplation I salve my sorrows, with applying the perfection of every object to the excellence of her qualities.'

'She is much beholding unto you,' quoth Aliena, 'and so much, that I have oft wished with myself, that if I should ever prove as amorous as Oenone, I might find as faithful a Paris as yourself.'

'How say you by this item, forester ?' quoth Ganymede, 'the fair shepherdess favours you, who is mistress of so many flocks. Leave off, man, the supposition of Rosalynde's love, whenas watching at her you rove beyond the moon, and cast your looks upon my mistress, who no doubt is as fair though not so royal ; one bird in the hand is worth two in the wood : better possess the love of Aliena than catch furiously at the shadow of Rosalynde.'

'I'll tell thee boy,' quoth Rosader, 'so is my fancy fixed on my Rosalynde, that were thy mistress as fair as Leda or

Danaë, whom Jove courted in transformed shapes, mine eyes would not vouch to entertain their beauties; and so hath love locked me in her perfections, that I had rather only contemplate in her beauties, than absolutely possess the excellence of any other.'

'Venus is to blame, forester, if having so true a servant of you, she reward you not with Rosalynde, if Rosalynde were more fairer than herself. But leaving this prattle, now I'll put you in mind of your promise about those sonnets, which you said were at home in your lodge.'

'I have them about me,' quoth Rosader, 'let us sit down, and then you shall hear what a poetical fury love will infuse into a man.' With that they sate down upon a green bank, shadowed with fig trees, and Rosader, fetching a deep sigh, read them this sonnet:

ROSADER'S SONNET

In sorrow's cell I laid me down to sleep,
  But waking woes were jealous of mine eyes,
They made them watch, and bend themselves to weep,
  But weeping tears their want could not suffice:
    Yet since for her they wept who guides my heart,
    They weeping smile, and triumph in their smart.

Of these my tears a fountain fiercely springs,
  Where Venus bains herself incensed with love,
Where Cupid bowseth his fair feathered wings;
  But I behold what pains I must approve.
    Care drinks it dry; but when on her I think,
    Love makes me weep it full unto the brink.

Meanwhile my sighs yield truce unto my tears,
  By them the winds increased and fiercely blow :
Yet when I sigh the flame more plain appears,
  And by their force with greater power doth glow :
    Amid these pains, all phoenix-like I thrive
    Since love, that yields me death, may life revive.

Rosader en esperance.

'Now, surely, forester,' quoth Aliena, 'when thou madest this sonnet, thou wert in some amorous quandary, neither too fearful as despairing of thy mistress' favours, nor too gleesome as hoping in thy fortunes.'

'I can smile,' quoth Ganymede, 'at the sonettos, canzones, madrigals, rounds and roundelays, that these pensive patients pour out when their eyes are more full of wantonness, than their hearts of passions. Then, as the fishers put the sweetest bait to the fairest fish, so these Ovidians, holding *amo* in their tongues, when their thoughts come at haphazard, write that they be rapt in an endless labyrinth of sorrow, when walking in the large lease of liberty, they only have their humours in their inkpot. If they find women so fond, that they will with such painted lures come to their lust, then they triumph till they be full-gorged with pleasures ; and then fly they away, like ramage kites, to their own content, leaving the tame fool, their mistress, full of fancy, yet without even a feather. If they miss, as dealing with some wary wanton, that wants not such a one as themselves, but spies their subtlety, they end their amours with a few feigned sighs ; and so their excuse is, their mistress is cruel, and they smother passions with patience. Such, gentle forester, we may deem you to be, that rather pass away the time here in these woods with writing amorets, than to be deeply enamoured, as you say, of your Rosalynde. If you be such a one, then I pray God, when you think your fortunes at the highest, and your desires to be most excellent, then that you may with Ixion embrace Juno in a cloud, and have nothing but a marble mistress to release your martyrdom; but if you be true and trusty, eye-pained and heart-sick, then accursed be Rosalynde if she prove cruel: for, forester, I flatter not, thou art worthy of as fair as she.' Aliena, spying the storm by the wind, smiled to see how Ganymede flew to the fist without any call; but Rosader, who took him flat for a shepherd's swain, made him this answer :

'Trust me, swain,' quoth Rosader, 'but my canzon was written in no such humour ; for mine eye and my heart are relatives, the one drawing fancy by sight, the other entertaining her by sorrow. If thou sawest my Rosaylnde, with what beauties nature hath favoured her, with what perfection the heavens hath graced her, with what qualities the gods have endued her, then wouldst thou say, there is none so fickle that could be fleeting unto her. If she had been Aeneas' Dido, had Venus and Juno both scolded him from Carthage, yet her excellence, despite of them, would have detained him at Tyre. If Phyllis had been as beauteous, or Ariadne as virtuous, or both as honourable and excellent as she, neither

G

had the filbert tree sorrowed in the death of despairing
Phyllis, nor the stars been graced with Ariadne, but
Demophoon and Theseus had been trusty to their paragons.
I will tell thee, swain, if with a deep insight thou couldst
pierce into the secret of my loves, and see what deep im-
pressions of her idea affection hath made in my heart, then
wouldst thou confess I were passing passionate, and no less
endued with admirable patience.'

'Why,' quoth Aliena, 'needs there patience in
love?'

'Or else in nothing,' quoth Rosader; 'for it is a restless
sore that hath no ease, a canker that still frets, a disease
that taketh away all hope of sleep. If then so many
sorrows, sudden joys, momentary pleasures, continual fears,
daily griefs, and nightly woes be found in love, then is
not he to be accounted patient that smothers all these
passions with silence?'

'Thou speakest by experience,' quoth Ganymede, 'and
therefore we hold all thy words for axioms. But is love
such a lingering malady?'

'It is,' quoth he, 'either extreme or mean, according to
the mind of the party that entertains it; for, as the weeds
grow longer untouched than the pretty flowers, and the flint
lies safe in the quarry when the emerald is suffering the
lapidary's tool, so mean men are freed from Venus' injuries,
when kings are environed with a labyrinth of her cares.
The whiter the lawn is, the deeper is the mole; the more

purer the chrysolite, the sooner stained; and such as have
their hearts full of honour, have their loves full of the greatest
sorrows.   But in whomsoever,' quoth Rosader, 'he fixeth his
dart, he never leaveth to assault him, till either he hath won
him to folly or fancy; for as the moon never goes without
the star Lunisequa, so a lover never goeth without the unrest
of his thoughts.   For proof you shall hear another fancy
of my making.'

'Now do, gentle forester,' quoth Ganymede; and with
that he read over this sonetto:

Rosader's second Sonetto

Turn I my looks unto the skies,
Love with his arrows wounds mine eyes;
If so I gaze upon the ground,
Love then in every flower is found.
Search I the shade to fly my pain,
He meets me in the shade again;
Wend I to walk in secret grove,
Even there I meet with sacred Love.
If so I bain me in the spring,
Even on the brink I hear him sing:
If so I meditate alone,
He will be partner of my moan.
If so I mourn he weeps with me,
And where I am there will he be.
Whenas I talk of Rosalynde
The god from coyness waxeth kind,
And seems in selfsame flames to fry
Because he loves as well as I.

Sweet Rosalynde, for pity rue;
For why, than Love I am more true:
He, if he speed, will quickly fly,
But in thy love I live and die.

' How like you this sonnet?' quoth Rosader.

'Marry,' quoth Ganymede, 'for the pen well, for the passion ill; for as I praise the one, I pity the other, in that thou shouldst hunt after a cloud, and love either without reward or regard.'

''Tis not her frowardness,' quoth Rosader, 'but my hard fortunes, whose destinies have crossed me with her absence; for did she feel my loves, she would not let me linger in these sorrows. Women, as they are fair, so they respect faith, and estimate more, if they be honourable, the will than the wealth, having loyalty the object whereat they aim their fancies. But leaving off these interparleys, you shall hear my last sonetto, and then you have heard all my poetry.' And with that he sighed out this:

ROSADER'S THIRD SONNET

Of virtuous love myself may boast alone,
    Since no suspect my service may attaint:
For perfect fair she is the only one,
    Whom I esteem for my belovèd saint.
        Thus, for my faith I only bear the bell,
        And for her fair she only doth excel.

Then let fond Petrarch shroud his Laura's praise,
    And Tasso cease to publish his affect,
Since mine the faith confirmed at all assays,
    And hers the fair, which all men do respect.

My lines her fair, her fair my faith assures;
Thus I by love, and love by me endures.

'Thus,' quoth Rosader, 'here is an end of my poems, but for all this no release of my passions ; so that I resemble him that in the depth of his distress hath none but the echo to answer him.'

Ganymede, pitying her Rosader, thinking to drive him out of this amorous melancholy, said that now the sun was in his meridional heat and that it was high noon, 'therefore we shepherds say, 'tis time to go to dinner ; for the sun and our stomachs are shepherds' dials.   Therefore, forester, if thou wilt take such fare as comes out of our homely scrips, welcome shall answer whatsoever thou wantest in delicates.'

Aliena took the entertainment by the end, and told Rosader he should be her guest.   He thanked them heartily, and sate with them down to dinner, where they had such cates as country state did allow them, sauced with such content, and such sweet prattle, as it seemed far more sweet than all their courtly junkets.

As soon as they had taken their repast, Rosader, giving them thanks for his good cheer, would have been gone ; but Ganymede, that was loath to let him pass out of her presence, began thus :

'Nay, forester,' quoth he, 'if thy business be not the greater, seeing thou sayest thou art so deeply in love, let me see how thou canst woo : I will represent Rosalynde, and thou shalt be as thou art, Rosader.   See in some amorous eclogue, how if Rosalynde were present, how thou couldst court her; and while we sing of love, Aliena shall tune her pipe and play us melody.'

'Content,' quoth Rosader, and Aliena, she, to show her willingness, drew forth a recorder, and began to wind it. Then the loving forester began thus:

THE WOOING ECLOGUE BETWIXT ROSALYNDE AND ROSADER

Rosader

I pray thee, nymph, by all the working words,
By all the tears and sighs that lovers know,
Or what or thoughts or faltering tongue affords,
I crave for mine in ripping up my woe.
Sweet Rosalynde, my love—would God, my love—
My life—would God, my life—aye, pity me!
Thy lips are kind, and humble like the dove,
And but with beauty pity will not be.
Look on mine eyes, made red with rueful tears,
From whence the rain of true remorse descendeth,
All pale in looks am I though young in years,
And nought but love or death my days befriendeth.
Oh let no stormy rigour knit thy brows,
Which love appointed for his mercy seat:
The tallest tree by Boreas' breath it bows;
The iron yields with hammer, and to heat.
    O Rosalynde, then be thou pitiful,
    For Rosalynde is only beautiful.

Rosalynde

Love's wantons arm their trait'rous suits with tears,
With vows, with oaths, with looks, with showers of gold;
But when the fruit of their affects appears,
The simple heart by subtle sleights is sold.

Thus sucks the yielding ear the poisoned bait,
Thus feeds the heart upon his endless harms,
Thus glut the thoughts themselves on self-deceit,
Thus blind the eyes their sight by subtle charms.
The lovely looks, the sighs that storm so sore,
The dew of deep-dissembled doubleness,
These may attempt, but are of power no more
Where beauty leans to wit and soothfastness.
    O Rosader, then be thou wittiful,
    For Rosalynde scorns foolish pitiful.

Rosader

I pray thee, Rosalynde, by those sweet eyes
That stain the sun in shine, the morn in clear,
By those sweet cheeks where Love encampèd lies
To kiss the roses of the springing year.
I tempt thee, Rosalynde, by ruthful plaints,
Not seasoned with deceit or fraudful guile,
But firm in pain, far more than tongue depaints,
Sweet nymph, be kind, and grace me with a smile.
So may the heavens preserve from hurtful food
Thy harmless flocks; so may the summer yield
The pride of all her riches and her good,
To fat thy sheep, the citizens of field.
Oh, leave to arm thy lovely brows with scorn:
The birds their beak, the lion hath his tail,
And lovers nought but sighs and bitter mourn,
The spotless fort of fancy to assail.
    O Rosalynde, then be thou pitiful,
    For Rosalynde is only beautiful.

Rosalynde

The hardened steel by fire is brought in frame.

Rosader

And Rosalynde, my love, than any wool more softer;
And shall not sighs her tender heart inflame?

Rosalynde

Were lovers true, maids would believe them ofter.

Rosader

Truth, and regard, and honour, guide my love.

Rosalynde

Fain would I trust, but yet I dare not try.

Rosader

Oh pity me, sweet nymph, and do but prove.

Rosalynde

I would resist, but yet I know not why.

Rosader

O Rosalynde, be kind, for times will change,
Thy looks ay nill be fair as now they be;
Thine age from beauty may thy looks estrange:
Ah, yield in time, sweet nymph, and pity me.

Rosalynde

O Rosalynde, thou must be pitiful,
For Rosader is young and beautiful.

Rosader

Oh, gain more great than kingdoms or a crown!

Rosalynde

Oh, trust betrayed if Rosader abuse me.

Rosader

First let the heavens conspire to pull me down
And heaven and earth as abject quite refuse me.
Let sorrows stream about my hateful bower,
And restless horror hatch within my breast:
Let beauty's eye afflict me with a lour,
Let deep despair pursue me without rest,
Ere Rosalynde my loyalty disprove,
Ere Rosalynde accuse me for unkind.

Rosalynde

Then Rosalynde will grace thee with her love,
Then Rosalynde will have thee still in mind.

Rosader

Then let me triumph more than Tithon's dear,
Since Rosalynde will Rosader respect:
Then let my face exile his sorry cheer,
And frolic in the comfort of affect;
   And say that Rosalynde is only pitiful,
   Since Rosalynde is only beautiful.

When thus they had finished their courting eclogue in such a familiar clause, Ganymede, as augur of some good fortunes to light upon their affections, began to be thus pleasant:

'How now, forester, have I not fitted your turn? have I not played the woman handsomely, and showed myself as

coy in grants as courteous in desires, and been as full of
suspicion as men of flattery? and yet to salve all, jumped I
not all up with the sweet union of love? Did not Rosalynde
content her Rosader?'

The forester at this smiling, shook his head, and folding
his arms made this merry reply:

'Truth, gentle swain, Rosader hath his Rosalynde; but
as Ixion had Juno, who, thinking to possess a goddess,
only embraced a cloud: in these imaginary fruitions of
fancy I resemble the birds that fed themselves with Zeuxis'
painted grapes; but they grew so lean with pecking at
shadows, that they were glad, with Aesop's cock, to scrape
for a barley cornel. So fareth it with me, who to feed
myself with the hope of my mistress's favours, sooth myself
in thy suits, and only in conceit reap a wished-for
content; but if my food be no better than such amorous
dreams, Venus at the year's end shall find me but a lean
lover. Yet do I take these follies for high fortunes, and
hope these feigned affections do divine some unfeigned end
of ensuing fancies.'

'And thereupon,' quoth Aliena, 'I'll play the priest: from
this day forth Ganymede shall call thee husband, and thou
shall call Ganymede wife, and so we'll have a marriage.'

'Content,' quoth Rosader, and laughed.

'Content,' quoth Ganymede, and changed as red as a
rose: and so with a smile and a blush, they made up this
jesting match, that after proved to a marriage in earnest,

Rosader full little thinking he had wooed and won his Rosalynde.

But all was well; hope is a sweet string to harp on, and therefore let the forester awhile shape himself to his shadow, and tarry fortune's leisure, till she may make a metamorphosis fit for his purpose. I digress; and therefore to Aliena, who said, the wedding was not worth a pin, unless there were some cheer, nor that bargain well made that was not stricken up with a cup of wine: and therefore she willed Ganymede to set out such cates as they had, and to draw out her bottle, charging the forester, as he had imagined his loves, so to conceit these cates to be a most sumptuous banquet, and to take a mazer of wine and to drink to his Rosalynde; which Rosader did, and so they passed away the day in many pleasant devices. Till at last Aliena perceived time would tarry no man, and that the sun waxed very low, ready to set, which made her shorten their amorous prattle, and end the banquet with a fresh carouse: which done, they all three arose, and Aliena broke off thus:

'Now, forester, Phoebus that all this while hath been partaker of our sports, seeing every woodman more fortunate in his loves than he in his fancies, seeing thou hast won Rosalynde when he could not woo Daphne, hides his head for shame and bids us adieu in a cloud. Our sheep, they poor wantons, wander towards their folds, as taught by nature their due times of rest, which tells us, forester, we must depart. Marry, though there were a marriage, yet I must

carry this night the bride with me, and to-morrow morning
if you meet us here, I'll promise to deliver you her as good
a maid as I find her.'

'Content,' quoth Rosader, ''tis enough for me in the night
to dream on love, that in the day am so fond to doat on love:
and so till to-morrow you to your folds, and I will to my
lodge.' And thus the forester and they parted.

He was no sooner gone, but Aliena and Ganymede went
and folded their flocks, and taking up their hooks, their bags,
and their bottles, hied homeward. By the way Aliena, to
make the time seem short, began to prattle with Ganymede
thus:

'I have heard them say, that what the fates forepoint, that
fortune pricketh down with a period; that the stars are
sticklers in Venus' court, and desire hangs at the heel of
destiny: if it be so, then by all probable conjectures, this
match will be a marriage: for if augurism be authentical,
or the divines' dooms principles, it cannot be but such a
shadow portends the issue of a substance, for to that end did
the gods force the conceit of this eclogue, that they might
discover the ensuing consent of your affections: so that ere
it be long, I hope, in earnest, to dance at your wedding.'

'Tush,' quoth Ganymede, 'all is not malt that is cast on the
kiln: there goes more words to a bargain than one: Love
feels no footing in the air, and fancy holds it slippery
harbour to nestle in the tongue: the match is not yet so
surely made, but he may miss of his market; but if fortune

be his friend, I will not be his foe: and so I pray you, gentle mistress Aliena, take it.'

'I take all things well,' quoth she, 'that is your content, and am glad Rosader is yours; for now I hope your thoughts will be at quiet; your eye that ever looked at love, will now lend a glance on your lambs, and then they will prove more buxom and you more blithe, for the eyes of the master feeds the cattle.'

As thus they were in chat, they spied old Corydon where he came plodding to meet them, who told them supper was ready, which news made them speed them home. Where we will leave them to the next morrow, and return to Saladyne.

All this while did poor Saladyne, banished from Bordeaux and the court of France by Torismond, wander up and down in the forest of Arden, thinking to get to Lyons, and so travel through Germany into Italy: but the forest being full of by-paths, and he unskilful of the country coast, slipped out of the way, and chanced up into the desert, not far from the place where Gerismond was, and his brother Rosader. Saladyne, weary with wandering up and down and hungry with long fasting, finding a little cave by the side of a thicket, eating such fruit as the forest did afford and contenting himself with such drink as nature had provided and thirst made delicate, after his repast he fell in a dead sleep. As thus he lay, a hungry lion came hunting down the edge of the grove for prey, and espying

Saladyne began to seize upon him: but seeing he lay still without any motion, he left to touch him, for that lions hate to prey on dead carcases; and yet desirous to have some food, the lion lay down and watched to see if he would stir. While thus Saladyne slept secure, fortune that was careful of her champion began to smile, and brought it so to pass, that Rosader, having stricken a deer that but lightly hurt fled through the thicket, came pacing down by the grove with a boar-spear in his hand in great haste. He spied where a man lay asleep, and a lion fast by him: amazed at this sight, as he stood gazing, his nose on the sudden bled, which made him conjecture it was some friend of his. Whereupon drawing more nigh, he might easily discern his visage, perceived by his physnomy that it was his brother Saladyne, which drave Rosader into a deep passion, as a man perplexed at the sight of so unexpected a chance, marvelling what should drive his brother to traverse those secret deserts, without any company, in such distress and forlorn sort. But the present time craved no such doubting ambages, for either he must resolve to hazard his life for his relief, or else steal away, and leave him to the cruelty of the lion. In which doubt he thus briefly debated with himself:

'Now, Rosader, fortune that long hath whipped thee with *Rosader's* nettles, means to salve thee with roses, and *meditation.* having crossed thee with many frowns, now she presents thee with the brightness of her favours. Thou that didst count thyself the most distressed of all men, mayest account thyself the most fortunate amongst men, if Fortune can make men happy, or sweet revenge be wrapped in a pleasing content. Thou seest Saladyne thine enemy, the worker of thy misfortunes, and the efficient cause of thine exile, subject to the cruelty of a merciless lion, brought into this misery by the gods, that they might seem just in revenging his rigour, and thy injuries. Seest thou not how the stars are in a favourable aspect, the planets in some pleasing conjunction, the fates agreeable to thy thoughts, and the destinies performers of thy desires, in that Saladyne shall die, and thou be free of his blood: he receive meed for his amiss, and thou erect his tomb with innocent hands. Now, Rosader, shalt thou return unto Bordeaux and enjoy thy possessions by birth, and his revenues by inheritance: now mayest thou triumph in love, and hang fortune's altars with garlands. For when Rosalynde hears of thy wealth, it will make her love thee the more willingly: for women's eyes are made of Chrysocoll, that is ever unperfect unless tempered with gold, and Jupiter soonest enjoyed Danaë, because he came to her in so rich a shower. Thus shall this lion, Rosader, end the life of a miserable man, and from distress raise thee to be most fortunate.' And with that, casting his boar-spear on his neck, away he began to trudge.

But he had not stepped back two or three paces, but a new motion stroke him to the very heart, that resting his boar-spear against his breast, he fell into this passionate humour :

'Ah, Rosader, wert thou the son of Sir John of Bordeaux, whose virtues exceeded his valour, and yet the most hardiest knight in all Europe? Should the honour of the father shine in the actions of the son, and wilt thou dishonour thy parentage, in forgetting the nature of a gentleman? Did not thy father at his last gasp breathe out this golden principle : Brothers' amity is like the drops of balsamum, that salveth the most dangerous sores? Did he make a large exhort unto concord, and wilt thou show thyself careless? O Rosader, what though Saladyne hath wronged thee, and made thee live an exile in the forest, shall thy nature be so cruel, or thy nurture so crooked, or thy thoughts so savage, as to suffer so dismal a revenge? What, to let him be devoured by wild beasts ! *Non sapit qui non sibi sapit* is fondly spoken in such bitter extremes. Lose not his life, Rosader, to win a world of treasure; for in having him thou hast a brother, and by hazarding for his life, thou gettest a friend, and reconcilest an enemy : and more honour shalt thou purchase by pleasuring a foe, than revenging a thousand injuries.'

With that his brother began to stir, and the lion to rouse himself, whereupon Rosader suddenly charged him with the boar-spear, and wounded the lion very sore at the first stroke. The beast feeling himself to have a mortal hurt, leapt at Rosader, and with his paws gave him a sore pinch on the breast, that he had almost fallen ; yet as a man most valiant, in whom the sparks of Sir John of Bordeaux remained, he recovered himself, and in short combat slew the lion, who at his death roared so loud that Saladyne awaked, and starting up, was amazed at the sudden sight of so monstrous a beast lying slain by him, and so sweet a gentleman wounded. He presently, as he was of a ripe conceit, began to conjecture that the gentleman had slain him in his defence. Whereupon, as a man in a trance, he stood staring on them both a good while, not knowing his brother, being in that disguise. At last he burst into these terms :

' Sir, whatsoever thou be, as full of honour thou must needs be by the view of thy present valour, I perceive thou hast redressed my fortunes by thy courage, and saved my life with thine own loss, which ties me to be thine in all humble service. Thanks thou shalt have as thy due, and more thou canst not have, for my ability denies me to perform a deeper debt. But if anyways it please thee to command me, use me as far as the power of a poor gentleman may stretch.'

Rosader, seeing he was unknown to his brother, wondered to hear such courteous words come from his crabbed nature ; but glad of such reformed nurture, he made this answer :

' I am, sir, whatsoever thou art, a forester and ranger of these walks, who, following my deer to the fall, was conducted hither by some assenting fate, that I might save thee, and disparage myself. For coming into this place, I saw thee asleep, and the lion watching thy awake, that at thy

H

rising he might prey upon thy carcase. At the first sight I conjectured thee a gentleman, for all men's thoughts ought to be favourable in imagination, and I counted it the part of a resolute man to purchase a stranger's relief, though with the loss of his own blood; which I have performed, thou seest, to mine own prejudice. If, therefore, thou be a man of such worth as I value thee by thy exterior lineaments, make discourse unto me what is the cause of thy present fortunes. For by the furrows in thy face thou seemest to be crossed with her frowns: but whatsoever, or howsoever, let me crave that favour, to hear the tragic cause of thy estate.'

Saladyne sitting down, and fetching a deep sigh, began thus:

'Although the discourse of my fortunes be the renewing of my sorrows, and the rubbing of the scar will open a fresh wound, yet that I may not prove ingrateful to so courteous a gentleman, I will rather sit down and sigh out my estate, than give any offence by smothering my grief with silence.

Saladyne's discourse to Rosader unknown.

Know therefore, sir, that I am of Bordeaux, and the son and heir of Sir John of Bordeaux, a man for his virtues and valour so famous, that I cannot think but the fame of his honours hath reached farther than the knowledge of his personage. The infortunate son of so fortunate a knight am I; my name, Saladyne; who succeeding my father in possessions, but not in qualities, having two brethren committed by my father at his death to my charge, with such

golden principles of brotherly concord, as might have pierced
like the Sirens' melody into any human ear. But I, with
Ulysses, became deaf against his philosophical harmony, and
made more value of profit than of virtue, esteeming gold
sufficient honour, and wealth the fittest title for a gentleman's
dignity. I set my middle brother to the university to be
a scholar, counting it enough if he might pore on a book
while I fed upon his revenues; and for the youngest, which
was my father's joy, young Rosader '— And with that, naming
of Rosader, Saladyne sate him down and wept.

'Nay, forward man,' quoth the forester, 'tears are the
unfittest salve that any man can apply for to cure sorrows, and
therefore cease from such feminine follies, as should drop out
of a woman's eye to deceive, not out of a gentleman's look to
discover his thoughts, and forward with thy discourse.'

'O sir,' quoth Saladyne, 'this Rosader that wrings tears
from mine eyes, and blood from my heart, was like my father
in exterior personage and in inward qualities; for in the
prime of his years he aimed all his acts at honour, and coveted
rather to die than to brook any injury unworthy a gentleman's
credit. I, whom envy had made blind, and covetousness
masked with the veil of self-love, seeing the palm tree grow
straight, thought to suppress it being a twig; but nature will
have her course, the cedar will be tall, the diamond bright,
the carbuncle glistering, and virtue will shine though it be
never so much obscured. For I kept Rosader as a slave, and
used him as one of my servile hinds, until age grew on, and

a secret insight of my abuse entered into his mind ; insomuch, that he could not brook it, but coveted to have what his father left him, and to live of himself.   To be short, sir, I repined at his fortunes, and he counterchecked me, not with ability but valour, until at last, by my friends and aid of such as followed gold more than right or virtue, I banished him from Bordeaux, and he, poor gentleman, lives no man knows where, in some distressed discontent.   The gods, not able to suffer such impiety unrevenged, so wrought, that the king picked a causeless quarrel against me in hope to have my lands, and so hath exiled me out of France for ever. Thus, thus, sir, am I the most miserable of all men, as having a blemish in my thoughts for the wrongs I proffered Rosader, and a touch in my state to be thrown from my proper possessions by injustice.   Passionate thus with many griefs, in penance of my former follies I go thus pilgrim-like to seek out my brother, that I may reconcile myself to him in all submission, and afterward wend to the Holy Land, to end my years in as many virtues as I have spent my youth in wicked vanities.'

Rosader, hearing the resolution of his brother Saladyne, began to compassionate his sorrows, and not able to smother the sparks of nature with feigned secrecy, he burst into these loving speeches :

'Then know, Saladyne,' quoth he, 'that thou hast met with Rosader, who grieves as much to see thy distress, as thyself to feel the burden of thy misery.'   Saladyne, casting

up his eye and noting well the physnomy of the forester, knew,
that it was his brother Rosader, which made him so bash and
blush at the first meeting, that Rosader was fain to recomfort
him, which he did in such sort, that he showed how highly
he held revenge in scorn.   Much ado there was between
these two brethren, Saladyne in craving pardon, and Rosader
in forgiving and forgetting all former injuries; the one submiss, the other courteous; Saladyne penitent and passionate,
Rosader kind and loving, that at length nature working an
union of their thoughts, they earnestly embraced, and fell
from matters of unkindness, to talk of the country life,
which Rosader so highly commended, that his brother began
to have a desire to taste of that homely content.   In this
humour Rosader conducted him to Gerismond's lodge, and
presented his brother to the king, discoursing the whole
matter how all had happened betwixt them.   The king looking upon Saladyne, found him a man of a most beautiful
personage, and saw in his face sufficient sparks of ensuing
honours, gave him great entertainment, and glad of their
friendly reconcilement, promised such favour as the poverty of
his estate might afford, which Saladyne gratefully accepted.
And so Gerismond fell to question of Torismond's life.   Saladyne briefly discoursed unto him his injustice and tyrannies,
with such modesty, although he had wronged him, that
Gerismond greatly praised the sparing speech of the young
gentleman.

Many questions passed, but at last Gerismond began with

a deep sigh to inquire if there were any news of the welfare of Alinda, or his daughter Rosalynde?

'None, sir,' quoth Saladyne, 'for since their departure they were never heard of.'

'Injurious fortune,' quoth the king, 'that to double the father's misery, wrongest the daughter with misfortunes!'

And with that, surcharged with sorrows, he went into his cell, and left Saladyne and Rosader, whom Rosader straight conducted to the sight of Adam Spencer. Who, seeing Saladyne in that estate, was in a brown study; but when he heard the whole matter, although he grieved for the exile of his master, yet he joyed that banishment had so reformed him, that from a lascivious youth he was proved a virtuous gentleman. Looking a longer while, and seeing what familiarity passed between them, and what favours were interchanged with brotherly affection, he said thus:

'Aye, marry, thus should it be; this was the concord that old Sir John of Bordeaux wished betwixt you. Now fulfil you those precepts he breathed out at his death, and in observing them, look to live fortunate and die honourable.'

'Well said, Adam Spencer,' quoth Rosader, 'but hast any victuals in store for us?'

'A piece of a red deer,' quoth he, 'and a bottle of wine.'

''Tis foresters' fare, brother,' quoth Rosader; and so they sate down and fell to their cates.

As soon as they had taken their repast, and had well dined, Rosader took his brother Saladyne by the hand, and showed him the pleasures of the forest, and what content they enjoyed in that mean estate. Thus for two or three days he walked up and down with his brother to show him all the commodities that belonged to his walk.

In which time he was missed of his Ganymede, who mused greatly, with Aliena, what should become of their forester. Somewhile they thought he had taken some word unkindly, and had taken the pet; then they imagined some new love had withdrawn his fancy, or happily that he was sick, or detained by some great business of Gerismond's, or that he had made a reconcilement with his brother, and so returned to Bordeaux.

These conjectures did they cast in their heads, but specially Ganymede, who, having love in her heart, proved restless, and half without patience, that Rosader wronged her with so long absence; for Love measures every minute, and thinks hours to be days, and days to be months, till they feed their eyes with the sight of their desired object. Thus perplexed lived poor Ganymede, while on a day, sitting with Aliena in a great dump, she cast up her eye, and saw where Rosader came pacing towards them with his forest bill on his neck. At that sight her colour changed, and she said to Aliena:

'See, mistress, where our jolly forester comes.'

'And you are not a little glad thereof,' quoth Aliena, 'your nose bewrays what porridge you love: the wind cannot be tied within his quarter, the sun shadowed with a veil, oil hidden in water, nor love kept out of a woman's looks : but no more of that, *Lupus est in fabula.*'

As soon as Rosader was come within the reach of her tongue's end, Aliena began thus :

' Why, how now, gentle forester, what wind hath kept you from hence ? that being so newly married, you have no more care of your Rosalynde, but to absent yourself so many days ? Are these the passions you painted out so in your sonnets and roundelays ? I see well hot love is soon cold, and that the fancy of men is like to a loose feather that wandereth in the air with the blast of every wind.'

' You are deceived, mistress,' quoth Rosader ; ' 'twas a copy of unkindness that kept me hence, in that, I being married, you carried away the bride ; but if I have given any occasion of offence by absenting myself these three days, I humbly sue for pardon, which you must grant of course, in that the fault is so friendly confessed with penance. But to tell you the truth, fair mistress and my good Rosalynde, my eldest brother by the injury of Torismond is banished from Bordeaux, and by chance he and I met in the forest.'

And here Rosader discoursed unto them what had happened betwixt them, which reconcilement made them glad, especially Ganymede. But Aliena, hearing of the tyranny of her father, grieved inwardly, and yet smothered all things with such secrecy, that the concealing was more sorrow than the conceit ; yet that her estate might be hid still, she made fair weather of it, and so let all pass.

Fortune, that saw how these parties valued not her deity, but held her power in scorn, thought to have a bout with them, and brought the matter to pass thus. Certain rascals that lived by prowling in the forest, who for fear of the provost marshal had caves in the groves and thickets to shroud themselves from his trains, hearing of the beauty of this fair shepherdess, Aliena, thought to steal her away, and to give her to the king for a present; hoping, because the king was a great lecher, by such a gift to purchase all their pardons, and therefore came to take her and her page away. Thus resolved, while Aliena and Ganymede were in this sad talk, they came rushing in, and laid violent hands upon Aliena and her page, which made them cry out to Rosader; who having the valour of his father stamped in his heart, thought rather to die in defence of his friends, than any way be touched with the least blemish of dishonour, and therefore dealt such blows amongst them with his weapon, as he did witness well upon their carcases that he was no coward. But as *Ne Hercules quidem contra duos*, so Rosader could not resist a multitude, having none to back him; so that he was not only rebated, but sore wounded, and Aliena and Ganymede had been quite carried away by these rascals, had not fortune, that meant to turn her frown into a favour, brought Saladyne that way by chance, who wandering to find out his brother's walk, encountered this crew: and seeing not only a shepherdess and her boy forced, but his brother wounded, he heaved up a forest bill he had on his neck, and the first he stroke had never after more need of the physician, redoubling his blows with such courage that the slaves were amazed at his valour. Rosader, espying his brother so fortunately arrived, and seeing how valiantly he behaved himself, though sore wounded rushed amongst them, and laid on such load, that some of the crew were slain, and the rest fled, leaving Aliena and Ganymede in the possession of Rosader and Saladyne.

Aliena after she had breathed awhile and was come to herself from this fear, looked about her, and saw where Ganymede was busy dressing up the wounds of the forester : but she cast her eye upon this courteous champion that had made so hot a rescue, and that with such affection, that she began to measure every part of him with favour, and in herself to commend his personage and his virtue, holding him for a resolute man, that durst assail such a troop of unbridled villains. At last, gathering her spirits together, she returned him these thanks :

' Gentle sir, whatsoever you be that have adventured your flesh to relieve our fortunes, as we hold you valiant so we esteem you courteous, and to have as many hidden virtues as you have manifest resolutions. We poor shepherds have no wealth but our flocks, and therefore can we not make requital with any great treasures ; but our recompense is thanks, and our rewards to her friends without feigning. For ransom, therefore, of this our rescue, you must content yourself to take such a kind gramercy as a poor shepherdess and her page may give, with promise, in what we may, never to prove ingrateful. For this gentleman that is hurt, young Rosader, he is our good neighbour and familiar acquaintance ; we'll pay him with smiles, and feed him with love-looks, and though he be never the fatter at the year's end, yet we'll so hamper him that he shall hold himself satisfied.'

Saladyne, hearing this shepherdess speak so wisely, began more narrowly to pry into her perfection, and to survey all her lineaments with a curious insight ; so long dallying in the flame of her beauty, that to his cost he found her to be most excellent. For love that lurked in all these broils to have a blow or two, seeing the parties at the gaze, encountered them both with such a veny, that the stroke pierced to the heart so deep as it could never after be rased out. At last, after he had looked so long, till Aliena waxed red, he returned her this answer :

' Fair shepherdess, if Fortune graced me with such good hap as to do you any favour, I hold myself as contented as if I had gotten a great conquest ; for the relief of distressed women is the special point that gentlemen are tied unto by honour. Seeing then my hazard to rescue your harms was rather duty than courtesy, thanks is more than belongs to the requital of such a favour. But lest I might seem either too coy or too careless of a gentlewoman's proffer, I will take your kind gramercy for a recompense.'

All this while that he spake, Ganymede looked earnestly upon him, and said :

'Truly, Rosader, this gentleman favours you much in the feature of your face.'

'No marvel,' quoth he, 'gentle swain, for 'tis my eldest brother Saladyne.'

'Your brother?' quoth Aliena, and with that she blushed, 'he is the more welcome, and I hold myself the more his debtor ; and for that he hath in my behalf done such a piece of service, if it please him to do me that honour, I will call him servant, and he shall call me mistress.'

'Content, sweet mistress,' quoth Saladyne, 'and when I forget to call you so, I will be unmindful of mine own self.'

'Away with these quirks and quiddities of love,' quoth Rosader, 'and give me some drink, for I am passing thirsty, and then will I home, for my wounds bleed sore, and I will have them dressed.'

Ganymede had tears in her eyes, and passions in her heart to see her Rosader so pained, and therefore stepped hastily to the bottle, and filling out some wine in a mazer, she spiced it with such comfortable drugs as she had about her, and gave it him, which did comfort Rosader, that rising, with the help of his brother, he took his leave of them, and went to his lodge. Ganymede, as soon as they were out of sight, led his flocks down to a vale, and there under the shadow of a beech tree sate down, and began to mourn the misfortunes of her sweetheart.

And Aliena, as a woman passing discontent, severing herself from her Ganymede, sitting under a limon tree, began to sigh out the passions of her new love, and to meditate with herself in this manner :

'Ay me! now I see, and sorrowing sigh to see, that Diana's laurels are harbours for Venus' doves; that there trace as well through the lawns wantons as *Aliena's* chaste ones; that Calisto, be she never so chary, *meditation.* will cast one amorous eye at courting Jove; that Diana herself will change her shape, but she will honour Love in a shadow; that maidens' eyes be they as hard as diamonds, yet Cupid hath drugs to make them more pliable than wax. See, Alinda, how Fortune and Love have interleagued themselves to be thy foes, and to make thee their subject, or else an abject, have inveigled thy sight with a most beautiful object. A-late thou didst hold Venus for a giglot, not a goddess, and now thou shalt be forced to sue suppliant to her deity. Cupid was a boy and blind; but, alas, his eye had aim enough to pierce thee to the heart. While I lived in the court I held love in contempt, and in high seats I had small desires. I knew not affection while I lived in dignity, nor could Venus countercheck me, as long as my fortune was majesty, and my thoughts honour; and shall I now be high in desires, when I am made low by destiny? I have heard them say, that Love looks not at low cottages, that Venus jets in robes not in rags, that Cupid flies so high, that he scorns to touch poverty with his heel. Tush, Alinda, these are but old wives' tales, and neither authentical precepts, nor infallible principles; for experience tells thee, that peasants have their passions as well as princes, that swains as they have their labours, so they have their amours, and Love lurks as soon about a sheepcote as a palace.

'Ah, Alinda, this day in avoiding a prejudice thou art fallen into a deeper mischief; being rescued from the robbers, thou art become captive to Saladyne: and what then? Women must love, or they must cease to live; and therefore did nature frame them fair, that they might be subjects to fancy. But perhaps Saladyne's eye is levelled upon a more seemlier saint. If it be so, bear thy passions with patience; say Love hath wronged thee, that hath not wrung him; and if he be proud in contempt, be thou rich in content, and rather die than discover any desire: for there is nothing more precious in a woman than to conceal love and to die modest. He is the son and heir of Sir John of Bordeaux, a youth comely enough. O Alinda, too comely, else hadst not thou been thus discontent; valiant, and that fettered thine eye; wise, else hadst thou not been now won; but for all these virtues banished by thy father, and therefore if he know thy parentage, he will hate the fruit for the tree, and condemn the young scion for the old stock. Well, howsoever, I must love, and whomsoever, I will; and, whatsoever betide, Aliena will think well of Saladyne, suppose he of me as he please.'

And with that fetching a deep sigh, she rise up, and went to Ganymede, who all this while sate in a great dump, fearing the imminent danger of her friend Rosader; but now

Aliena began to comfort her, herself being overgrown with sorrows, and to recall her from her melancholy with many pleasant persuasions. Ganymede took all in the best part, and so they went home together after they had folded their flocks, supping with old Corydon, who had provided their cates. He, after supper, to pass away the night while bedtime, began a long discourse, how Montanus, the young shepherd that was in love with Phoebe, could by no means obtain any favour at her hands, but, still pained in restless passions, remained a hopeless and perplexed lover.

'I would I might,' quoth Aliena, 'once see that Phoebe. Is she so fair that she thinks no shepherd worthy of her beauty? or so froward that no love nor loyalty will content her? or so coy that she requires a long time to be wooed? or so foolish that she forgets that like a fop she must have a large harvest for a little corn?'

'I cannot distinguish,' quoth Corydon, 'of these nice qualities; but one of these days I'll bring Montanus and her down, that you may both see their persons, and note their passions; and then where the blame is, there let it rest. But this I am sure,' quoth Corydon, 'if all maidens were of her mind, the world would grow to a mad pass; for there would be great store of wooing and little wedding, many words and little worship, much folly and no faith.'

At this sad sentence of Corydon, so solemnly brought forth, Aliena smiled, and because it waxed late, she and her page went to bed, both of them having fleas in their ears to keep them awake; Ganymede for the hurt of her Rosader, and Aliena for the affection she bore to Saladyne. In this discontented humour they passed away the time, till falling on sleep, their senses at rest, Love left them to their quiet slumbers, which were not long. For as soon as Phoebus rose from his Aurora, and began to mount him in the sky, summoning plough-swains to their handy labour, Aliena arose, and going to the couch where Ganymede lay, awakened her page, and said the morning was far spent, the dew small, and time called them away to their folds.

'Ah, ah!' quoth Ganymede, 'is the wind in that door? then in faith I perceive that there is no diamond so hard but will yield to the file, no cedar so strong but the wind will shake, nor any mind so chaste but love will change. Well, Aliena, must Saladyne be the man, and will it be a match? Trust me, he is fair and valiant, the son of a worthy knight, whom if he imitate in perfection, as he represents him in proportion, he is worthy of no less than Aliena. But he is an exile. What then? I hope my mistress respects the virtues not the wealth, and measures the qualities not the substance. Those dames that are like Danaë, that like Jove in no shape but in a shower of gold, I wish them husbands with much wealth and little wit, that the want of the one may blemish the abundance of the other. It should, my Aliena, stain the honour of a shepherd's life to set the end of passions upon pelf. Love's eyes looks not so low as gold; there is no fees to be paid in Cupid's courts; and in elder time, as Corydon hath told me, the shepherds' love-gifts were apples and chestnuts, and then their desires were loyal, and their thoughts constant.   But now

        Quaerenda pecunia primum, post nummos virtus.

And the time is grown to that which Horace in his Satires wrote on :

                 omnis enim res
  Virtus fama decus divina humanaque pulchris
  Divitiis parent: quas qui construxerit ille
  Clarus erit, fortis, justus.   Sapiensne?   Etiam et rex
  Et quicquid volet—

But, Aliena, let it not be so with thee in thy fancies, but respect his faith and there an end.'

Aliena, hearing Ganymede thus forward to further Saladyne in his affections, thought she kissed the child for the nurse's sake, and wooed for him that she might please Rosader, made this reply :

'Why, Ganymede, whereof grows this persuasion?   Hast thou seen love in my looks, or are mine eyes grown so amorous, that they discover some new-entertained fancies?   If thou measurest my thoughts by my countenance, thou mayest prove as ill a physiognomer, as the lapidary that aims at the secret virtues of the topaz by the exterior shadow of the stone.   The operation of the agate is not known by the strakes, nor the diamond prized by his

                                      I

brightness, but by his hardness. The carbuncle that shineth most is not ever the most precious; and the apothecaries choose not flowers for their colours, but for their virtues. Women's faces are not always calendars of fancy, nor do their thoughts and their looks ever agree; for when their eyes are fullest of favours, then are they oft most empty of desire; and when they seem to frown at disdain, then are they most forward to affection. If I be melancholy, then, Ganymede, 'tis not a consequence that I am entangled with the perfection of Saladyne. But seeing fire cannot be hid in the straw, nor love kept so covert but it will be spied, what should friends conceal fancies? Know, my Ganymede, the beauty and valour, the wit and prowess of Saladyne hath fettered Aliena so far, as there is no object pleasing to her eyes but the sight of Saladyne; and if Love have done me justice to wrap his thoughts in the folds of my face, and that he be as deeply enamoured as I am passionate, I tell thee, Ganymede, there shall not be much wooing, for she is already won, and what needs a longer battery.'

'I am glad,' quoth Ganymede, 'that it shall be thus proportioned, you to match with Saladyne, and I with Rosader: thus have the Destinies favoured us with some pleasing aspect, that have made us as private in our loves, as familiar in our fortunes.'

With this Ganymede start up, made her ready, and went into the fields with Aliena, where unfolding their flocks, they sate them down under an olive tree, both of them amorous, and yet diversely affected; Aliena joying in the excellence of Saladyne, and Ganymede sorrowing for the wounds of her Rosader, not quiet in thought till she might hear of his health. As thus both of them sate in their dumps, they might espy where Corydon came running towards them, almost out of breath with his haste.

' What news with you,' quoth Aliena, ' that you come in such post ? '

' Oh, mistress,' quoth Corydon, ' you have a long time desired to see Phoebe, the fair shepherdess whom Montanus loves; so now if you please, you and Ganymede, but to walk with me to yonder thicket, there shall you see Montanus and her sitting by a fountain, he courting with his country ditties, and she as coy as if she held love in disdain.'

The news were so welcome to the two lovers, that up they rose, and went with Corydon. As soon as they drew nigh the thicket, they might espy where Phoebe sate, the fairest shepherdess in all Arden, and he the frolickest swain in the whole forest, she in a petticoat of scarlet, covered with a green mantle, and to shroud her from the sun, a chaplet of roses, from under which appeared a face full of nature's excellence, and two such eyes as might have amated a greater man than Montanus. At gaze upon the gorgeous nymph sat the shepherd, feeding his eyes with her favours, wooing with such piteous looks, and courting with such deep-strained sighs, as would have made Diana herself to have been compassionate. At last, fixing his looks on the riches of her

face, his head on his hand, and his elbow on his knee, he
sung this mournful ditty:

Montanus' Sonnet

A turtle sate upon a leaveless tree,
    Mourning her absent fere
    With sad and sorry cheer:
About her wondering stood
    The citizens of wood,
And whilst her plumes she rents
And for her love laments,
    The stately trees complain them,
    The birds with sorrow pain them.
Each one that doth her view
    Her pain and sorrows rue;
But were the sorrows known
    That me hath overthrown,
Oh how would Phoebe sigh if she did look on me!

The lovesick Polypheme, that could not see,
    Who on the barren shore
    His fortunes doth deplore,
And melteth all in moan
    For Galatea gone,
And with his piteous cries
Afflicts both earth and skies,
    And to his woe betook
    Doth break both pipe and hook,
For whom complains the morn,
    For whom the sea-nymphs mourn,
Alas, his pain is nought;
    For were my woe but thought,
Oh how would Phoebe sigh if she did look on me!

> Beyond compare my pain ;
>   Yet glad am I,
> If gentle Phoebe deign
>   To see her Montan die.

After this, Montanus felt his passions so extreme, that he fell into this exclamation against the injustice of Love :'

> Hélas, tyran, plein de rigueur,
> Modère un peu ta violence:
> Que te sert si grande dépense?
> C'est trop de flammes pour un cœur.
> Épargnez en une étincelle,
> Puis fais ton effort d'émouvoir,
> La fière qui ne veut point voir,
> En quel feu je brûle pour elle.
> Exécute, Amour, ce dessein,
> Et rabaisse un peu son audace :
> Son cœur ne doit être de glace,
> Bien qu'elle ait de neige le sein.

Montanus ended his sonnet with such a volley of sighs, and such a stream of tears, as might have moved any but Phoebe to have granted him favour. But she, measuring all his passions with a coy disdain, and triumphing in the poor shepherd's pathetical humours, smiling at his martyrdom as though love had been no malady, scornfully warbled out this sonnet :

Phoebe's Sonnet, a Reply to Montanus' Passion

Down a down,
　　Thus Phyllis sung,
　　　　By fancy once distressed ;
Whoso by foolish love are stung
　　Are worthily oppressed.
　　　　And so sing I. With a down, down, &c.

When Love was first begot,
　　And by the mover's will
Did fall to human lot
　　His solace to fulfil,
Devoid of all deceit,
　　A chaste and holy fire
Did quicken man's conceit,
　　And women's breast inspire.
The gods that saw the good
　　That mortals did approve,
With kind and holy mood
　　Began to talk of Love.

　　Down a down,
　　　　Thus Phyllis sung
　　　　　　By fancy once distressed, &c.

But during this accord,
　　A wonder strange to hear,
Whilst Love in deed and word
　　Most faithful did appear,
False-semblance came in place,
　　By Jealousy attended,
And with a double face
　　Both love and fancy blended ;

Which made the gods forsake,
And men from fancy fly,
And maidens scorn a make,
Forsooth, and so will I.

Down a down,
Thus Phyllis sung,
By fancy once distressed ;
Who so by foolish love are stung
Are worthily oppressed.
And so sing I.
With down a down, a down down, a down a.

Montanus, hearing the cruel resolution of Phoebe, was so overgrown with passions, that from amorous ditties he fell flat into these terms :

'Ah, Phoebe,' quoth he, 'whereof art thou made, that thou regardest not my malady? Am I so hateful an object that thine eyes condemn me for an abject? or so base, that thy desires cannot stoop so low as to lend me a gracious look? My passions are many, my loves more, my thoughts loyalty, and my fancy faith : all devoted in humble devoir to the service of Phoebe ; and shall I reap no reward for such fealties? The swain's daily labours is quit with the evening's hire, the ploughman's toil is eased with the hope of corn, what the ox sweats out at the plough he fatteneth at the crib ; but infortunate Montanus hath no salve for his sorrows, nor any hope of recompense for the hazard of his perplexed passions. If, Phoebe, time may plead the proof of my truth, twice seven winters have I loved fair Phoebe :

if constancy be a cause to farther my suit, Montanus' thoughts have been sealed in the sweet of Phoebe's excellence, as far from change as she from love : if outward passions may discover inward affections, the furrows in my face may decipher the sorrows of my heart, and the map of my looks the griefs of my mind. Thou seest, Phoebe, the tears of despair have made my cheeks full of wrinkles, and my scalding sighs have made the air echo her pity conceived in my plaints : Philomele hearing my passions, hath left her mournful tunes to listen to the discourse of my miseries. I have portrayed in every tree the beauty of my mistress, and the despair of my loves. What is it in the woods cannot witness my woes ? and who is it would not pity my plaints ? Only Phoebe. And why ? Because I am Montanus, and she Phoebe : I a worthless swain, and she the most excellent of all fairies. Beautiful Phoebe ! oh, might I say pitiful, then happy were I, though I tasted but one minute of that good hap. Measure Montanus not by his fortunes but by his loves, and balance not his wealth but his desires, and lend but one gracious look to cure a heap of disquieted cares. If not, ah ! if Phoebe cannot love, let a storm of frowns end the discontent of my thoughts, and so let me perish in my desires, because they are above my deserts : only at my death this favour cannot be denied me, that all shall say Montanus died for love of hard-hearted Phoebe.'

At these words she filled her face full of frowns, and made him this short and sharp reply :

'Importunate shepherd, whose loves are lawless, because
restless, are thy passions so extreme that thou canst not
conceal them with patience? or art thou so folly-sick, that
thou must needs be fancy-sick, and in thy affection tied
to such an exigent, as none serves but Phoebe? Well, sir,
if your market may be made no where else, home again, for
your mart is at the fairest. Phoebe is no lettuce for your
lips, and her grapes hangs so high, that gaze at them you may,
but touch them you cannot. Yet, Montanus, I speak not
this in pride, but in disdain; not that I scorn thee, but that
I hate love; for I count it as great honour to triumph over
fancy as over fortune. Rest thee content therefore, Montanus:
cease from thy loves, and bridle thy looks, quench the
sparkles before they grow to a further flame; for in loving
me thou shalt live by loss, and what thou utterest in words
are all written in the wind. Wert thou, Montanus, as
fair as Paris, as hardy as Hector, as constant as Troilus, as
loving as Leander, Phoebe could not love, because she cannot
love at all: and therefore if thou pursue me with Phoebus, I
must fly with Daphne.'

Ganymede, overhearing all these passions of Montanus,
could not brook the cruelty of Phoebe, but starting from
behind the bush said:

'And if, damsel, you fled from me, I would transform
you as Daphne to a bay, and then in contempt trample your
branches under my feet.'

Phoebe at this sudden reply was amazed, especially when

she saw so fair a swain as Ganymede; blushing therefore, she would have been gone, but that he held her by the hand, and prosecuted his reply thus:

'What, shepherdess, so fair and so cruel? Disdain beseems not cottages, nor coyness maids; for either they be condemned to be too proud, or too froward. Take heed, fair nymph, that in despising love, you be not overreached with love, and in shaking off all, shape yourself to your own shadow, and so with Narcissus prove passionate and yet unpitied. Oft have I heard, and sometimes have I seen, high disdain turned to hot desires. Because thou art beautiful be not so coy: as there is nothing more fair, so there is nothing more fading; as momentary as the shadows which grows from a cloudy sun. Such, my fair shepherdess, as disdain in youth desire in age, and then are they hated in the winter, that might have been loved in the prime. A wrinkled maid is like to a parched rose, that is cast up in coffers to please the smell, not worn in the hand to content the eye. There is no folly in love to *had I wist*, and therefore be ruled by me. Love while thou art young, least thou be disdained when thou art old. Beauty nor time cannot be recalled, and if thou love, like of Montanus; for if his desires are many, so his deserts are great.'

Phœbe all this while gazed on the perfection of Ganymede, as deeply enamoured on his perfection as Montanus inveigled with hers; for her eye made survey of his excellent feature, which she found so rare, that she thought the ghost of Adonis had been leaped from Elysium in the shape of a swain.   When she blushed at her own folly to look so long on a stranger, she mildly made answer to Ganymede thus :

'I cannot deny, sir, but I have heard of Love, though I never felt love ; and have read of such a goddess as Venus, though I never saw any but her picture ; and, perhaps '— and with that she waxed red and bashful, and withal silent ; which Ganymede perceiving, commended in herself the bashfulness of the maid, and desired her to go forward.

'And perhaps, sir,' quoth she, 'mine eye hath been more prodigal to-day than ever before '—and with that she stayed again, as one greatly passionate and perplexed.

Aliena seeing the hare through the maze, bade her forward with her prattle, but in vain ; for at this abrupt period she broke off, and with her eyes full of tears, and her face covered with a vermilion dye, she sate down and sighed. Whereupon Aliena and Ganymede, seeing the shepherdess in such a strange plight, left Phoebe with her Montanus, wishing her friendly that she would be more pliant to Love, lest in penance Venus joined her to some sharp repentance. Phoebe made no reply, but fetched such a sigh, that Echo made relation of her plaint, giving Ganymede such an adieu with a piercing glance, that the amorous girl-boy perceived Phoebe was pinched by the heel.

But leaving Phoebe to the follies of her new fancy, and Montanus to attend upon her, to Saladyne, who all this last night could not rest for the remembrance of Aliena ; insomuch that he framed a sweet conceited sonnet to content his humour, which he put in his bosom, being requested by his brother Rosader to go to Aliena and Ganymede, to signify unto them that his wounds were not dangerous. A more happy message could not happen to Saladyne, that taking his forest bill on his neck, he trudgeth in all haste towards the plains where Aliena's flocks did feed, coming just to the place when they returned from Montanus and Phoebe. Fortune so conducted this jolly forester, that he encountered them and Corydon, whom he presently saluted in this manner:

'Fair shepherdess, and too fair, unless your beauty be tempered with courtesy, and the lineaments of the face graced with the lowliness of mind, as many good fortunes to you and your page, as yourselves can desire or I imagine. My brother Rosader, in the grief of his green wounds still mindful of his friends, hath sent me to you with a kind salute, to show that he brooks his pains with the more patience, in that he holds the parties precious in whose defence he received the prejudice. The report of your welfare will be a great comfort to his distempered body and distressed thoughts, and therefore he sent me with a strict charge to visit you.'

'And you,' quoth Aliena, 'are the more welcome in that you are messenger from so kind a gentleman, whose pains we compassionate with as great sorrow as he brooks them with grief ; and his wounds breeds in us as many passions as in

him extremities, so that what disquiet he feels in body we
partake in heart, wishing, if we might, that our mishap might
salve his malady.   But seeing our wills yields him little ease,
our orisons are never idle to the gods for his recovery.'

'I pray, youth,' quoth Ganymede with tears in his
eyes, 'when the surgeon searched him, held he his wounds
dangerous?'

'Dangerous,' quoth Saladyne, 'but, not mortal; and the
sooner to be cured, in that his patient is not impatient of any
pains: whereupon my brother hopes within these ten days
to walk abroad and visit you himself.'

'In the meantime,' quoth Ganymede, 'say his Rosalynde
commends her to him, and bids him be of good cheer.'

'I know not,' quoth Saladyne, 'who that Rosalynde is, but
whatsoever she is, her name is never out of his mouth, but
amidst the deepest of his passions he useth Rosalynde as a
charm to appease all sorrows with patience; insomuch that
I conjecture my brother is in love, and she some paragon
that holds his heart perplexed, whose name he oft records
with sighs, sometimes with tears, straight with joy, then
with smiles; as if in one person love had lodged a Chaos of
confused passions.   Wherein I have noted the variable disposition of fancy, that like the polype in colours, so it
changeth into sundry humours, being, as it should seem, a
combat mixed with disquiet and a bitter pleasure wrapped in
a sweet prejudice, like to the Sinople tree, whose blossoms
delight the smell, and whose fruit infects the taste.'

'By my faith,' quoth Aliena, 'sir, you are deep read in love, or grows your insight into affection by experience? Howsoever, you are a great philosopher in Venus' principles, else could you not discover her secret aphorisms. But, sir, our country amours are not like your courtly fancies, nor is our wooing like your suing; for poor shepherds never plain them till love pain them, where the courtier's eyes is full of passions, when his heart is most free from affection; they court to discover their eloquence, we woo to ease our sorrows; every fair face with them must have a new fancy sealed with a forefinger kiss and a far-fetched sigh, we here love one and live to that one so long as life can maintain love, using few ceremonies because we know few subtleties, and little eloquence for that we lightly account of flattery; only faith and troth, that's shepherds' wooing; and, sir, how like you of this?'

'So,' quoth Saladyne, 'as I could tie myself to such love.'

'What, and look so low as a shepherdess, being the son of Sir John of Bordeaux? Such desires were a disgrace to your honours.' And with that surveying exquisitely every part of him, as uttering all these words in a deep passion, she espied the paper in his bosom; whereupon growing jealous that it was some amorous sonnet, she suddenly snatched it out of his bosom and asked if it were any secret. She was bashful, and Saladyne blushed, which she preceiving, said:

'Nay then, sir, if you wax red, my life for yours 'tis some love-matter. I will see your mistress' name, her praises, and your passions.' And with that she looked on it, which was written to this effect:

SALADYNE'S SONNET

If it be true that heaven's eternal course
With restless sway and ceaseless turning glides;
If air inconstant be, and swelling source
Turn and returns with many fluent tides;
   If earth in winter summer's pride estrange,
   And nature seemeth only fair in change;

If it be true that our immortal spright,
Derived from heavenly pure, in wand'ring still,
In novelty and strangeness doth delight,
And by discoverent power discerneth ill;
   And if the body for to work his best
   Doth with the seasons change his place of rest;

Whence comes it that, enforced by furious skies,
I change both place and soil, but not my heart,
Yet salve not in this change my maladies?
Whence grows it that each object works my smart?
   Alas, I see my faith procures my miss,
   And change in love against my nature is.

Et florida pungunt.

Aliena having read over his sonnet, began thus pleasantly to descant upon it:

'I see, Saladyne,' quoth she, 'that as the sun is no sun without his brightness, nor the diamond accounted for precious unless it be hard, so men are not men unless they be in love; and their honours are measured by their amours, not their

labours, counting it more commendable for a gentleman to be
full of fancy, than full of virtue.   I had thought

Otia si tollas, periere Cupidinis arcus,
Contemptaeque jacent et sine luce faces.

But I see Ovid's axiom is not authentical, for even labour
hath her loves, and extremity is no pumice-stone to rase out
fancy.   Yourself exiled from your wealth, friends, and
country by Torismond, sorrows enough to suppress affections, yet amidst the depth of these extremities, love will
be lord, and show his power to be more predominant than
fortune.   But I pray you, sir, if without offence I may crave
it, are they some new thoughts, or some old desires?'

Saladyne, that now saw opportunity pleasant, thought to
strike while the iron was hot, and therefore taking Aliena
by the hand, sate down by her; and Ganymede, to give
them leave to their loves, found herself busy about the
folds, whilst Saladyne fell into this prattle with Aliena:

'Fair mistress, if I be blunt in discovering my affections,
and use little eloquence in levelling out my loves, I appeal
for pardon to your own principles, that say, shepherds use
few ceremonies, for that they acquaint themselves with few
subtleties.   To frame myself, therefore, to your country
fashion with much faith and little flattery, know, beautiful
shepherdess, that whilst I lived in the court I knew not
love's cumber, but I held affection as a toy, not as a malady;
using fancy as the Hyperborei do their flowers, which they

wear in their bosom all day, and cast them in the fire for
fuel at night.   I liked all, because I loved none, and who
was most fair, on her I fed mine eye, but as charily as the
bee, that as soon as she hath sucked honey from the rose,
flies straight to the next marigold.   Living thus at mine
own list, I wondered at such as were in love, and when I
read their passions, I took them only for poems that flowed
from the quickness of the wit, not the sorrows of the heart.
But now, fair nymph, since I became a forester, Love hath
taught me such a lesson that I must confess his deity and
dignity, and say as there is nothing so precious as beauty, so
there is nothing more piercing than fancy.   For since first I
arrived at this place, and mine eye took a curious survey of
your excellence, I have been so fettered with your beauty
and virtue, as, sweet Aliena, Saladyne without further circumstance loves Aliena.   I could paint out my desires with long
ambages ; but seeing in many words lies mistrust, and that
truth is ever naked, let this suffice for a country wooing,
Saladyne loves Aliena, and none but Aliena.'

Although these words were most heavenly harmony in
the ears of the shepherdess, yet to seem coy at the first
courting, and to disdain love howsoever she desired love, she
made this reply :

'Ah, Saladyne, though I seem simple, yet I am more
subtle than to swallow the hook because it hath a painted
bait : as men are wily so women are wary, especially if they
have that wit by others' harms to beware.   Do we not

know, Saladyne, men's tongues are like Mercury's pipe, that
can enchant Argus with an hundred eyes, and their words
as prejudicial as the charms of Circes, that transform men
into monsters. If such Sirens sing, we poor women had
need stop our ears, lest in hearing we prove so foolish
hardy as to believe them, and so perish in trusting much and
suspecting little. Saladyne, *piscator ictus sapit*, he that hath
been once poisoned and afterwards fears not to bowse of
every potion, is worthy to suffer double penance. Give
me leave then to mistrust, though I do not condemn.
Saladyne is now in love with Aliena, he a gentleman of
great parentage, she a shepherdess of mean parents; he
honourable and she poor? Can love consist of contrarieties?
Will the falcon perch with the kestrel, the lion harbour
with the wolf? Will Venus join robes and rags together,
or can there be a sympathy between a king and a beggar?
Then, Saladyne, how can I believe thee that love should
unite our thoughts, when fortune hath set such a difference
between our degrees? But suppose thou likest Aliena's
beauty: men in their fancy resemble the wasp, which scorns
that flower from which she hath fetched her wax; playing
like the inhabitants of the island Tenerifa, who, when
they have gathered the sweet spices, use the trees for fuel;
so men, when they have glutted themselves with the fair of
women's faces, hold them for necessary evils, and wearied
with that which they seemed so much to love, cast away
fancy as children do their rattles, and loathing that which

so deeply before they liked; especially such as take love in a minute and have their eyes attractive, like jet, apt to entertain any object, are as ready to let it slip again.'

Saladyne, hearing how Aliena harped still upon one string, which was the doubt of men's constancy, he broke off her sharp invective thus:

'I grant, Aliena,' quoth he, 'many men have done amiss in proving soon ripe and soon rotten; but particular instances infer no general conclusions, and therefore I hope what others have faulted in shall not prejudice my favours. I will not use sophistry to confirm my love, for that is subtlety; nor long discourses lest my words might be thought more than my faith: but if this will suffice, that by the honour of a gentleman I love Aliena, and woo Aliena, not to crop the blossoms and reject the tree, but to consummate my faithful desires in the honourable end of marriage.'

At the word marriage Aliena stood in a maze what to answer, fearing that if she were too coy, to drive him away with her disdain, and if she were too courteous, to discover the heat of her desires. In a dilemma thus what to do, at last this she said:

'Saladyne, ever since I saw thee, I favoured thee; I cannot dissemble my desires, because I see thou dost faithfully manifest thy thoughts, and in liking thee I love thee so far as mine honour holds fancy still in suspense; but if I knew thee as virtuous as thy father, or as well qualified as thy brother Rosader, the doubt should be quickly decided:

but for this time to give thee an answer, assure thyself
this, I will either marry with Saladyne, or still live a virgin.'

And with this they strained one another's hand ; which
Ganymede espying, thinking he had had his mistress long
enough at shrift, said :

'What, a match or no ? '

'A match,' quoth Aliena, 'or else it were an ill market.'

'I am glad,' quoth Ganymede. 'I would Rosader were
well here to make up a mess.'

'Well remembered,' quoth Saladyne ; 'I forgot I left my
brother Rosader alone, and therefore lest being solitary he
should increase his sorrows, I will haste me to him. May it
please you, then, to command me any service to him, I am
ready to be a dutiful messenger.'

'Only at this time commend me to him,' quoth Aliena,
'and tell him, though we cannot pleasure him we pray for
him.'

'And forget not,' quoth Ganymede, 'my commendations ;
but say to him that Rosalynde sheds as many tears from her
heart as he drops of blood from his wounds, for the sorrow
of his misfortunes, feathering all her thoughts with disquiet,
till his welfare procure her content. Say thus, good Saladyne,
and so farewell.'

He having his message, gave a courteous adieu to them
both, especially to Aliena, and so playing loath to depart,
went to his brother. But Aliena, she perplexed and yet
joyful, passed away the day pleasantly, still praising the

perfection of Saladyne, not ceasing to chat of her new love till evening drew on; and then they, folding their sheep, went home to bed. Where we leave them and return to Phoebe.

Phoebe, fired with the uncouth flame of love, returned to her father's house, so galled with restless passions, as now she began to acknowledge, that as there was no flower so fresh but might be parched with the sun, no tree so strong but might be shaken with a storm, so there was no thought so chaste, but time armed with love could make amorous; for she that held Diana for the goddess of her devotion, was now fain to fly to the altar of Venus, as suppliant now with prayers, as she was forward before with disdain. As she lay in her bed, she called to mind the several beauties of young Ganymede; first his locks, which being amber-hued, passeth the wreath that Phoebus puts on to make his front glorious; his brow of ivory was like the seat where love and majesty sits enthroned to enchain fancy; his eyes as bright as the burnishing of the heaven, darting forth frowns with disdain and smiles with favour, lightning such looks as would inflame desire, were she wrapped in the circle of the frozen zone; in his cheeks the vermilion teinture of the rose flourished upon natural alabaster, the blush of the morn and Luna's silver show were so lively portrayed, that the Troyan that fills out wine to Jupiter was not half so beautiful; his face was full of pleasance, and all the rest of his lineaments proportioned with such excellence, as Phoebe was fettered in the sweetness of his feature. The idea of these perfections tumbling in her mind made the poor shepherdess so perplexed, as feeling a pleasure tempered with intolerable pains, and yet a disquiet mixed with a content, she rather wished to die than to live in this amorous anguish. But wishing is little worth in such extremes, and therefore was she forced to pine in her malady, without any salve for her sorrows. Reveal it she durst not, as daring in such matters to make none her secretary; and to conceal it, why, it doubled her grief; for as fire suppressed grows to the greater flame, and the current stopped to the more violent stream, so love smothered wrings the heart with the deeper passions.

Perplexed thus with sundry agonies, her food began to fail, and the disquiet of her mind began to work a distemperature of her body, that, to be short, Phoebe fell extreme sick, and so sick as there was almost left no recovery of health. Her father, seeing his fair Phoebe thus distressed, sent for his friends, who sought by medicine to cure, and by counsel to pacify, but all in vain; for although her body was feeble through long fasting, yet she did *magis aegrotare animo quam corpore.* Which her friends perceived and sorrowed at, but salve it they could not.

The news of her sickness was bruited abroad through all the forest, which no sooner came to Montanus' ear, but he, like a madman, came to visit Phoebe. Where sitting by her bedside he began his exordium with so many tears and sighs, that she, perceiving the extremity of his sorrows, began now as a lover to pity them, although Ganymede held her from redressing them. Montanus craved to know the cause of her sickness, tempered with secret plaints, but she answered him, as the rest, with silence, having still the form of Ganymede in her mind, and conjecturing how she might reveal her loves. To utter it in words she found herself too bashful; to discourse by any friend she would not trust any in her amours; to remain thus perplexed still and conceal all, it was a double death. Whereupon, for her last refuge, she resolved to write unto Ganymede, and therefore desired Montanus to absent himself a while, but not to depart, for she would see if she could steal a nap. He was no sooner gone out of the chamber, but reaching to her standish, she took pen and paper, and wrote a letter to this effect:

'Phoebe to Ganymede wisheth what she wants herself.

Fair shepherd—and therefore is Phoebe infortunate, because thou art so fair—although hitherto mine eyes were adamants to resist love, yet I no sooner saw thy face, but they became amorous to entertain love; more devoted to fancy than before they were repugnant to affection, addicted to the one by nature and drawn to the other by beauty: which, being rare and made the more excellent by many virtues, hath so snared the freedom of Phoebe, as she rests at thy mercy, either to be made the most fortunate of all maidens, or the most miserable of all women.   Measure not, Ganymede, my loves by my wealth, nor my desires by my degrees ; but think my thoughts as full of faith, as thy face of amiable favours.   Then, as thou knowest thyself most beautiful, suppose me most constant.   If thou deemest me hard-hearted because I hated Montanus, think I was forced to it by fate ; if thou sayest I am kind-hearted because so lightly I love thee at the first look, think I was driven to it by destiny, whose influence, as it is mighty, so is it not to be resisted.   If my fortunes were anything but infortunate love, I would strive with fortune : but he that wrests against the will of Venus, seeks to quench fire with oil, and to thrust out one thorn by putting in another.   If then, Ganymede, love enters at the eye, harbours in the heart, and will neither be driven out with physic nor reason, pity me, as one whose malady hath no salve but from thy sweet self, whose grief hath no ease but through thy grant ; and think I am a virgin who is deeply wronged when I am forced to woo, and conjecture love to be strong, that is more forcible than nature.   Thus distressed unless by thee eased, I expect either to live fortunate by thy favour, or die miserable by thy denial.   Living in hope.   Farewell.

She that must be thine,

or not be at all,

Phoebe.'

To this letter she annexed this sonnet :

Sonetto

My boat doth pass the straits
   of seas incensed with fire,
Filled with forgetfulness;
   amidst the winter's night,
A blind and careless boy,
   brought up by fond desire,
Doth guide me in the sea
   of sorrow and despite.

For every oar he sets
   a rank of foolish thoughts,
And cuts, instead of wave,
   a hope without distress;
The winds of my deep sighs,
   that thunder still for noughts,
Have split my sails with fear,
   with care and heaviness.

A mighty storm of tears,
   a black and hideous cloud,
A thousand fierce disdains
   do slack the halyards oft;
Till ignorance do pull,
   and error hale the shrouds,
No star for safety shines,
   no Phoebe from aloft.

    Time hath subdued art,
      and joy is slave to woe:
    Alas, Love's guide, be kind!
      what, shall I perish so?

This letter and the sonnet being ended, she could find no

fit messenger to send it by, and therefore she called in
Montanus, and entreated him to carry it to Ganymede.
Although poor Montanus saw day at a little hole, and did
perceive what passion pinched her, yet, that he might seem
dutiful to his mistress in all service, he dissembled the
matter, and became a willing messenger of his own martyrdom. And so, taking the letter, went the next morn very
early to the plains where Aliena fed her flocks, and there
he found Ganymede, sitting under a pomegranate tree,
sorrowing for the hard fortunes of her Rosader. Montanus
saluted him, and according to his charge delivered Ganymede
the letters, which, he said, came from Phoebe. At this the
wanton blushed, as being abashed to think what news
should come from an unknown shepherdess; but taking the
letters, unripped the seals, and read over the discourse of
Phoebe's fancies. When she had read and over-read them
Ganymede began to smile, and looking on Montanus, fell
into a great laughter, and with that called Aliena, to whom
she showed the writings. Who, having perused them,
conceited them very pleasantly, and smiled to see how love
had yoked her, who before would not stoop to the lure;
Aliena whispering Ganymede in the ear, and saying, ' Knew
Phoebe what want there were in thee to perform her will,
and how unfit thy kind is to be kind to her, she would be
more wise, and less enamoured; but leaving that, I pray thee
let us sport with this swain.' At that word Ganymede,
turning to Montanus, began to glance at him thus:

'I pray thee, tell me, shepherd, by those sweet thoughts and pleasing sighs that grow from my mistress' favours, art thou in love with Phoebe?'

'Oh, my youth,' quoth Montanus, 'were Phoebe so far in love with me, my flocks would be more fat and their master more quiet; for through the sorrows of my discontent grows the leanness of my sheep.'

'Alas, poor swain,' quoth Ganymede, 'are thy passions so extreme or thy fancy so resolute, that no reason will blemish the pride of thy affection, and rase out that which thou strivest for without hope?'

'Nothing can make me forget Phoebe, while Montanus forget himself; for those characters which true love hath stamped, neither the envy of time nor fortune can wipe away.'

'Why but, Montanus,' quoth Ganymede, 'enter with a deep insight into the despair of thy fancies, and thou shalt see the depth of thine own follies; for, poor man, thy progress in love is a regress to loss, swimming against the stream with the crab, and flying with Apis Indica against wind and weather. Thou seekest with Phoebus to win Daphne, and she flies faster than thou canst follow: thy desires soar with the hobby, but her disdain reacheth higher than thou canst make wing. I tell thee, Montanus, in courting Phoebe, thou barkest with the wolves of Syria against the moon, and rovest at such a mark, with thy thoughts, as is beyond the pitch of thy bow, praying to Love, when Love is pitiless, and thy malady remediless. For proof, Montanus, read these letters, wherein thou shalt see thy great follies and little hope.'

With that Montanus took them and perused them, but with such sorrow in his looks, as they betrayed a source of confused passions in his heart; at every line his colour changed, and every sentence was ended with a period of sighs.

At last, noting Phoebe's extreme desire toward Ganymede and her disdain towards him, giving Ganymede the letter, the shepherd stood as though he had neither won nor lost. Which Ganymede perceiving wakened him out of his dream thus:

'Now, Montanus, dost thou see thou vowest great service and obtainest but little reward; but in lieu of thy loyalty, she maketh thee, as Bellerophon, carry thine own bane. Then drink not willingly of that potion wherein thou knowest is poison; creep not to her that cares not for thee. What, Montanus, there are many as fair as Phoebe, but most of all more courteous than Phoebe. I tell thee, shepherd, favour is love's fuel; then since thou canst not get that, let the flame vanish into smoke, and rather sorrow for a while than repent thee for ever.'

'I tell thee, Ganymede,' quoth Montanus, 'as they which are stung with the scorpion, cannot be recovered but by the scorpion, nor he that was wounded with Achilles' lance be cured but with the same truncheon, so Apollo was fain to cry out that love was only eased with love, and fancy healed

by no medicine but favour.   Phoebus had herbs to heal all
hurts but this passion; Circes had charms for all chances
but for affection, and Mercury subtle reasons to refel all
griefs but love.   Persuasions are bootless, reason lends no
remedy, counsel no comfort, to such whom fancy hath
made resolute; and therefore though Phoebe loves Ganymede,
yet Montanus must honour none but Phoebe.'

'Then,' quoth Ganymede, 'may I rightly term thee a
despairing lover, that livest without joy, and lovest without
hope.   But what shall I do, Montanus, to pleasure thee ?   Shall
I despise Phoebe, as she disdains thee ? '

'Oh,' quoth Montanus, 'that were to renew my griefs,
and double my sorrows; for the sight of her discontent
were the censure of my death.   Alas, Ganymede ! though I
perish in my thoughts, let not her die in her desires.   Of
all passions, love is most impatient: then let not so fair
a creature as Phoebe sink under the burden of so deep
a distress.   Being lovesick, she is proved heartsick, and
all for the beauty of Ganymede.   Thy proportion hath
entangled her affection, and she is snared in the beauty of
thy excellence.   Then, sith she loves thee so dear, mislike
not her deadly.   Be thou paramour to such a paragon : she
hath beauty to content thine eye, and flocks to enrich thy
store.   Thou canst not wish for more than thou shalt win by
her ; for she is beautiful, virtuous and wealthy, three deep
persuasions to make love frolic.'

Aliena seeing Montanus cut it against the hair, and plead

that Ganymede ought to love Phoebe, when his only life was
the love of Phoebe, answered him thus :

'Why, Montanus, dost thou further this motion, seeing
if Ganymede marry Phoebe thy market is clean marred ? '

'Ah, mistress,' quoth he, 'so hath love taught me to honour
Phoebe, that I would prejudice my life to pleasure her, and
die in despair rather than she should perish for want. It
shall suffice me to see her contented, and to feed mine eye
on her favour. If she marry, though it be my martyrdom,
yet if she be pleased I will brook it with patience, and
triumph in mine own stars to see her desires satisfied.
Therefore, if Ganymede be as courteous as he is beautiful,
let him show his virtues in redressing Phoebe's miseries.'
And this Montanus pronounced with such an assured countenance, that it amazed both Aliena and Ganymede to see the
resolution of his loves ; so that they pitied his passions and
commended his patience, devising how they might by any
subtlety get Montanus the favour of Phoebe. Straight, as
women's heads are full of wiles, Ganymede had a fetch to
force Phoebe to fancy the shepherd, malgrado the resolution
of her mind : he prosecuted his policy thus :

'Montanus,' quoth he, 'seeing Phoebe is so forlorn, lest
I might be counted unkind in not salving so fair a creature,
I will go with thee to Phoebe, and there hear herself in
word utter that which she hath discoursed with her pen ; and
then, as love wills me, I will set down my censure. I will
home by our house, and send Corydon to accompany Aliena.'

Montanus seemed glad of this determination and away they go towards the house of Phoebe

When they drew nigh to the cottage, Montanus ran before, and went in and told Phoebe that Ganymede was at the door. This word 'Ganymede,' sounding in the ears of Phoebe, drave her into such an ecstasy for joy, that rising up in her bed, she was half revived, and her wan colour began to wax red; and with that came Ganymede in, who saluted Phoebe with such a courteous look, that it was half a salve to her sorrows. Sitting him down by her bedside, he questioned about her disease, and where the pain chiefly held her? Phoebe looking as lovely as Venus in her night-gear, tainting her face with as ruddy a blush as Clytia did when she bewrayed her loves to Phoebus, taking Ganymede by the hand began thus:

'Fair shepherd, if love were not more strong than nature, or fancy the sharpest extreme, my immodesty were the more, and my virtues the less; for nature hath framed women's eyes bashful, their hearts full of fear, and their tongues full of silence; but love, that imperious love, where his power is predominant, then he perverts all, and wresteth the wealth of nature to his own will: an instance in myself, fair Ganymede, for such a fire hath he kindled in my thoughts, that to find ease for the flame, I was forced to pass the bounds of modesty, and seek a salve at thy hands for my harms. Blame me not if I be overbold for it is thy beauty, and if I be too forward it is fancy, and the deep insight into thy virtues that makes me thus fond; for let me say in a word what may be contained in a volume, Phoebe loves Ganymede.'

At this she held down her head and wept, and Ganymede rose as one that would suffer no fish to hang on his fingers, made this reply:

'Water not thy plants, Phoebe, for I do pity thy plaints, nor seek not to discover thy loves in tears, for I conjecture thy truth by thy passions: sorrow is no salve for loves, nor sighs no remedy for affection. Therefore frolic, Phoebe; for if Ganymede can cure thee, doubt not of recovery. Yet this let me say without offence, that it grieves me to thwart Montanus in his fancies, seeing his desires have been so resolute, and his thoughts so loyal. But thou allegest that thou art forced from him by fate: so I tell thee, Phoebe, either some star or else some destiny fits my mind, rather with Adonis to die in chase than be counted a wanton on Venus' knee. Although I pity thy martyrdom, yet I can grant no marriage; for though I held thee fair, yet mine eye is not fettered. Love grows not, like the herb Spattana, to his perfection in one night, but creeps with the snail, and yet at last attains to the top. *Festina lente*, especially in love, for momentary fancies are oft-times the fruits of follies. If, Phoebe, I should like thee as the Hyperborei do their dates, which banquet with them in the morning and throw them away at night, my folly should be great, and thy repentance more. Therefore I will have time to turn my thoughts, and my loves shall grow up as the watercresses, slowly, but with a deep root. Thus, Phoebe, thou mayest see I disdain not, though I desire not; remaining indifferent till time and love makes me resolute. Therefore, Phoebe, seek not to suppress affection, and with the love of Montanus quench the remembrance of Ganymede; strive thou to hate me as I seek to like of thee, and ever have the duties of Montanus in thy mind, for I promise thee thou mayest have one more wealthy, but not more loyal.' These words were corrosives to the perplexed Phoebe, that sobbing out sighs, and straining out tears, she blubbered out these words :

'And shall I then have no salve of Ganymede but suspense, no hope but a doubtful hazard, no comfort, but be posted off to the will of time ? Justly have the gods balanced my fortunes, who, being cruel to Montanus, found Ganymede as unkind to myself; so in forcing him perish for love, I shall die myself with overmuch love.'

'I am glad,' quoth Ganymede, 'you look into your own faults, and see where your shoe wrings you, measuring now the pains of Montanus by your own passions.'

'Truth,' quoth Phoebe, 'and so deeply I repent me of my frowardness toward the shepherd, that could I cease to love Ganymede, I would resolve to like Montanus.'

'What, if I can with reason persuade Phoebe to mislike of Ganymede, will she then favour Montanus ?'

'When reason,' quoth she, 'doth quench that love I owe

L

to thee, then will I fancy him; conditionally, that if my love can be suppressed with no reason, as being without reason Ganymede will only wed himself to Phoebe.'

'I grant it, fair shepherdess,' quoth he; 'and to feed thee with the sweetness of hope, this resolve on: I will never marry myself to woman but unto thyself.'

And with that Ganymede gave Phoebe a fruitless kiss, and such words of comfort, that before Ganymede departed she arose out of her bed, and made him and Montanus such cheer, as could be found in such a country cottage; Ganymede in the midst of their banquet rehearsing the promises of either in Montanus' favour, which highly pleased the shepherd. Thus, all three content, and soothed up in hope, Ganymede took his leave of his Phoebe and departed, leaving her a contented woman, and Montanus highly pleased. But poor Ganymede, who had her thoughts on her Rosader, when she called to remembrance his wounds, filled her eyes full of tears, and her heart full of sorrows, plodded to find Aliena at the folds, thinking with her presence to drive away her passions. As she came on the plains she might espy where Rosader and Saladyne sate with Aliena under the shade; which sight was a salve to her grief, and such a cordial unto her heart, that she tripped alongst the lawns full of joy.

At last Corydon, who was with them, spied Ganymede, and with that the clown rose, and, running to meet him, cried:

' O sirrah, a match, a match ! our mistress shall be married on Sunday.'

Thus the poor peasant frolicked it before Ganymede, who coming to the crew saluted them all, and especially Rosader, saying that he was glad to see him so well recovered of his wounds.

' I had not gone abroad so soon,' quoth Rosader, ' but that I am bidden to a marriage, which, on Sunday next, must be solemnized between my brother and Aliena. I see well where love leads delay is loathsome, and that small wooing serves where both the parties are willing.'

' Truth,' quoth Ganymede ; ' but a happy day should it be, if Rosader that day might be married to Rosalynde.'

' Ah, good Ganymede,' quoth he, ' by naming Rosalynde, renew not my sorrows ; for the thought of her perfections is the thrall of my miseries.'

' Tush, be of good cheer, man,' quoth Ganymede : ' I have a friend that is deeply experienced in negromancy and magic ; what art can do shall be acted for thine advantage. I will cause him to bring in Rosalynde, if either France or any bordering nation harbour her ; and upon that take the faith of a young shepherd.'

Aliena smiled to see how Rosader frowned, thinking that Ganymede had jested with him. But, breaking off from those matters, the page, somewhat pleasant, began to discourse unto them what had passed between him and Phoebe ; which, as they laughed, so they wondered at, all confessing that

there is none so chaste but love will change. Thus they
passed away the day in chat, and when the sun began to set
they took their leaves and departed; Aliena providing for
their marriage day such solemn cheer and handsome robes
as fitted their country estate, and yet somewhat the better, in
that Rosader had promised to bring Gerismond thither as a
guest. Ganymede, who then meant to discover herself before
her father, had made her a gown of green, and a kirtle of
the finest sendal, in such sort that she seemed some heavenly
nymph harboured in country attire.

Saladyne was not behind in care to set out the nuptials,
nor Rosader unmindful to bid guests, who invited Gerismond
and all his followers to the feast, who willingly granted,
so that there was nothing but the day wanting to this
marriage.

In the meanwhile, Phoebe being a bidden guest made herself as gorgeous as might be to please the eye of Ganymede;
and Montanus suited himself with the cost of many of his
flocks to be gallant against the day, for then was Ganymede to give Phoebe an answer of her loves, and Montanus
either to hear the doom of his misery, or the censure of
his happiness. But while this gear was a-brewing, Phoebe
passed not one day without visiting her Ganymede, so far
was she wrapped in the beauties of this lovely swain. Much
prattle they had, and the discourse of many passions, Phoebe
wishing for the day, as she thought, of her welfare, and
Ganymede smiling to think what unexpected events would

fall out at the wedding. In these humours the week went away, that at last Sunday came.

No sooner did Phoebus' henchman appear in the sky, to give warning that his master's horses should be trapped in his glorious coach, but Corydon, in his holiday suit, marvellous seemly, in a russet jacket, welted with the same and faced with red worsted, having a pair of blue chamlet sleeves, bound at the wrists with four yellow laces, closed before very richly with a dozen of pewter buttons; his hose was of grey kersey, with a large slop barred overthwart the pocket-holes with three fair guards, stitched of either side with red thread; his stock was of the own, sewed close to his breech, and for to beautify his hose, he had trussed himself round with a dozen of new-threaden points of medley colour: his bonnet was green, whereon stood a copper brooch with the picture of Saint Denis; and to want nothing that might make him amorous in his old days, he had a fair shirt-band of fine lockram, whipped over with Coventry blue of no small cost. Thus attired, Corydon bestirred himself as chief stickler in these actions, and had strowed all the house with flowers, that it seemed rather some of Flora's choice bowers than any country cottage.

Thither repaired Phoebe with all the maids of the forest, to set out the bride in the most seemliest sort that might be; but howsoever she helped to prank out Aliena, yet her eye was still on Ganymede, who was so neat in a suit of grey, that he seemed Endymion when he won Luna with his looks,

or Paris when he played the swain to get the beauty of the
nymph Oenone.   Ganymede, like a pretty page, waited on
his mistress Aliena, and overlooked that all was in a readiness
against the bridegroom should come ; who, attired in a forester's
suit, came accompanied with Gerismond and his brother
Rosader early in the morning ; where arrived, they were
solemnly entertained by Aliena and the rest of the country
swains ; Gerismond very highly commending the fortunate
choice of Saladyne, in that he had chosen a shepherdess,
whose virtues appeared in her outward beauties, being no
less fair than seeming modest.   Ganymede coming in, and
seeing her father, began to blush, nature working affects by
her secret effects.   Scarce could she abstain from tears to
see her father in so low fortunes, he that was wont to sit in
his royal palace, attended on by twelve noble peers, now
to be contented with a simple cottage, and a troop of revel-
ling woodmen for his train.   The consideration of his fall
made Ganymede full of sorrows ; yet, that she might triumph
over fortune with patience, and not any way dash that merry
day with her dumps, she smothered her melancholy with a
shadow of mirth, and very reverently welcomed the king,
not according to his former degree, but to his present estate,
with such diligence as Gerismond began to commend the
page for his exquisite person and excellent qualities.

As thus the king with his foresters frolicked it among the
shepherds, Corydon came in with a fair mazer full of cider,
and presented it to Gerismond with such a clownish salute
that he began to smile, and took it of the old shepherd very

kindly, drinking to Aliena and the rest of her fair maids, amongst whom Phoebe was the foremost. Aliena pledged the king, and drunk to Rosader; so the carouse went round from him to Phoebe, &c. As they were thus drinking and ready to go to church, came in Montanus, apparelled all in tawny, to signify that he was forsaken; on his head he wore a garland of willow, his bottle hanged by his side, whereon was painted despair, and on his sheep-hook hung two sonnets, as labels of his loves and fortunes.

Thus attired came Montanus in, with his face as full of grief as his heart was of sorrows, showing in his countenance the map of extremities. As soon as the shepherds saw him, they did him all the honour they could, as being the flower of all the swains in Arden; for a bonnier boy was there not seen since that wanton wag of Troy that kept sheep in Ida. He, seeing the king, and guessing it to be Gerismond, did him all the reverence his country courtesy could afford; insomuch that the king, wondering at his attire, began to question what he was. Montanus overhearing him, made this reply:

'I am, sir,' quoth he, 'Love's swain, as full of inward discontents as I seem fraught with outward follies. Mine eyes like bees delight in sweet flowers, but sucking their full on the fair of beauty, they carry home to the hive of my heart far more gall than honey, and for one drop of pure dew, a ton full of deadly Aconiton. I hunt with the fly to pursue the eagle, that flying too nigh the sun, I perish with the sun; my thoughts are above my reach, and my desires more than my fortunes, yet neither greater than my loves. But daring with Phaëthon, I fall with Icarus, and seeking to pass the mean, I die for being so mean; my night-sleeps are waking slumbers, as full of sorrows as they be far from rest; and my days' labours are fruitless amours, staring at a star and stumbling at a straw, leaving reason to follow after repentance; yet every passion is a pleasure though it pinch, because love hides his wormseed in figs, his poisons in sweet potions, and shadows prejudice with the mask of pleasure. The wisest counsellors are my deep discontents, and I hate that which should salve my harm, like the patient which stung with the Tarantula loathes music, and yet the disease incurable but by melody. Thus, sir, restless I hold myself remediless, as loving without either reward or regard, and yet loving because there is none worthy to be loved but the mistress of my thoughts. And that I am as full of passions as I have discoursed in my plaints, sir, if you please, see my sonnets, and by them censure of my sorrows.'

These words of Montanus brought the king into a great wonder, amazed as much at his wit as his attire, insomuch that he took the papers off his hook, and read them to this effect:

Montanus' first Sonnet

Alas! how wander I amidst these woods
  Whereas no day-bright shine doth find access;
But where the melancholy fleeting floods,
  Dark as the night, my night of woes express.

Disarmed of reason, spoiled of nature's goods,
  Without redress to salve my heaviness
    I walk, whilst thought, too cruel to my harms,
    With endless grief my heedless judgment charms.

My silent tongue assailed by secret fear,
  My traitorous eyes imprisoned in their joy,
My fatal peace devoured in feignèd cheer,
  My heart enforced to harbour in annoy,
My reason robbed of power by yielding ear,
  My fond opinions slave to every toy.
    O Love! thou guide in my uncertain way,
    Woe to thy bow, thy fire, the cause of my decay.

                              Et florida pungunt.

When the king had read this sonnet he highly commended
the device of the shepherd, that could so wittily wrap his
passions in a shadow, and so covertly conceal that which
bred his chiefest discontent; affirming, that as the least
shrubs have their tops, the smallest hairs their shadows,
so the meanest swains had their fancies, and in their kind
were as chary of love as a king. Whetted on with this
device, he took the second and read it: the effects were
these :

MONTANUS' SECOND SONNET

When the Dog
Full of rage,
  With his ireful eyes
  Frowns amidst the skies,

The shepherd, to assuage
   The fury of the heat,
   Himself doth safely seat
By a fount
Full of fair,
   Where a gentle breath,
   Mounting from beneath,
Tempereth the air.
There his flocks
Drink their fill,
   And with ease repose,
   Whilst sweet sleep doth close
Eyes from toilsome ill.
But I burn
Without rest,
   No defensive power
   Shields from Phoebe's lour;
Sorrow is my best.
Gentle Love,
Lour no more;
   If thou wilt invade
   In the secret shade,
Labour not so sore.
I myself
And my flocks,
   They their love to please,
   I myself to ease,
Both leave the shady oaks;
   Content to burn in fire,
   Sith Love doth so desire.

Et florida pungunt.

Gerismond, seeing the pithy vein of those sonnets, began
to make further inquiry what he was. Whereupon Rosader

discoursed unto him the love of Montanus to Phoebe, his great loyalty and her deep cruelty, and how in revenge the gods had made the curious nymph amorous of young Ganymede. Upon this discourse the king was desirous to see Phoebe, who being brought before Gerismond by Rosader, shadowed the beauty of her face with such a vermilion teinture, that the king's eyes began to dazzle at the purity of her excellence. After Gerismond had fed his looks awhile upon her fair, he questioned with her why she rewarded Montanus' love with so little regard, seeing his deserts were many, and his passions extreme. Phoebe, to make reply to the king's demand, answered thus :

' Love, sir, is charity in his laws, and whatsoever he sets down for justice, be it never so unjust, the sentence cannot be reversed ; women's fancies lend favours not ever by desert, but as they are enforced by their desires ; for fancy is tied to the wings of fate, and what the stars decree, stands for an infallible doom.   I know Montanus is wise, and women's ears are greatly delighted with wit, as hardly escaping the charm of a pleasant tongue, as Ulysses the melody of the Sirens.   Montanus is beautiful, and women's eyes are snared in the excellence of objects, as desirous to feed their looks with a fair face, as the bee to suck on a sweet flower. Montanus is wealthy, and an ounce of *give me* persuades a woman more than a pound of *hear me*.   Danaë was won with a golden shower, when she could not be gotten with all the entreaties of Jupiter.   I tell you, sir, the string of a woman's heart reacheth to the pulse of her hand ; and let a man rub that with gold, and 'tis hard but she will prove his heart's gold.   Montanus is young, a great clause in fancy's court ; Montanus is virtuous, the richest argument that love yields ; and yet knowing all these perfections, I praise them and wonder at them, loving the qualities, but not affecting the person, because the destinies have set down a contrary censure.   Yet Venus, to add revenge, hath given me wine of the same grape, a sip of the same sauce, and firing me with the like passion, hath crossed me with as ill a penance ; for I am in love with a shepherd's swain, as coy to me as I am cruel to Montanus, as peremptory in disdain as I was perverse in desire ; and that is,' quoth she, 'Aliena's page, young Ganymede.'

Gerismond, desirous to prosecute the end of these passions, called in Ganymede, who, knowing the case, came in graced with such a blush, as beautified the crystal of his face with a ruddy brightness.   The king noting well the physnomy of Ganymede, began by his favours to call to mind the face of his Rosalynde, and with that fetched a deep sigh.   Rosader, that was passing familiar with Gerismond, demanded of him why he sighed so sore.

'Because Rosader,' quoth he, 'the favour of Ganymede puts me in mind of Rosalynde.'

At this word Rosader sighed so deeply, as though his heart would have burst.

'And what's the matter,' quoth Gerismond, 'that you quite me with such a sigh ? '

'Pardon me, sir,' quoth Rosader, 'because I love none but Rosalynde.'

'And upon that condition,' quoth Gerismond, 'that Rosalynde were here, I would this day make up a marriage betwixt her and thee.'

At this Aliena turned her head and smiled upon Ganymede, and she could scarce keep countenance. Yet she salved all with secrecy; and Gerismond, to drive away his dumps, questioned with Ganymede, what the reason was he regarded not Phoebe's love, seeing she was as fair as the wanton that brought Troy to ruin. Ganymede mildly answered:

'If I should affect the fair Phoebe, I should offer poor Montanus great wrong to win that from him in a moment, that he hath laboured for so many months. Yet have I promised to the beautiful shepherdess to wed myself never to woman except unto her; but with this promise, that if I can by reason suppress Phoebe's love towards me, she shall like of none but of Montanus.'

'To that,' quoth Phoebe, 'I stand; for my love is so far beyond reason, as will admit no persuasion of reason.'

'For justice,' quoth he, 'I appeal to Gerismond.'

'And to his censure will I stand,' quoth Phoebe.

'And in your victory,' quoth Montanus, 'stands the hazard of my fortunes; for if Ganymede go away with conquest, Montanus is in conceit love's monarch; if Phoebe win, then am I in effect most miserable.'

'We will see this controversy,' quoth Gerismond, 'and then

we will to church.   Therefore, Ganymede, let us hear your argument.'

'Nay, pardon my absence a while,' quoth she, 'and you shall see one in store.'

In went Ganymede and dressed herself in woman's attire, having on a gown of green, with kirtle of rich sendal, so quaint, that she seemed Diana triumphing in the forest; upon her head she wore a chaplet of roses, which gave her such a grace that she looked like Flora perked in the pride of all her flowers. Thus attired came Rosalynde in, and presented herself at her father's feet, with her eyes full of tears, craving his blessing, and discoursing unto him all her fortunes, how she was banished by Torismond, and how ever since she lived in that country disguised.

Gerismond, seeing his daughter, rose from his seat and fell upon her neck, uttering the passions of his joy in watery plaints, driven into such an ecstasy of content, that he could not utter one word. At this sight, if Rosader was both amazed and joyful, I refer myself to the judgment of such as have experience in love, seeing his Rosalynde before his face whom so long and deeply he had affected. At last Gerismond recovered his spirits, and in most fatherly terms entertained his daughter Rosalynde, after many questions demanding of her what had passed between her and Rosader ?

'So much, sir,' quoth she, 'as there wants nothing but your grace to make up the marriage.'

'Why, then,' quoth Gerismond, 'Rosader take her: she is thine, and let this day solemnize both thy brother's and thy nuptials.' Rosader beyond measure content, humbly thanked the king, and embraced his Rosalynde, who turning to Phoebe, demanded if she had shown sufficient reason to suppress the force of her loves.

'Yea,' quoth Phoebe, 'and so great a persuasive, that if it please you, madame, and Aliena to give us leave, Montanus and I will make this day the third couple in marriage.'

She had no sooner spake this word, but Montanus threw away his garland of willow, his bottle, where was painted despair, and cast his sonnets in the fire, showing himself as frolic as Paris when he handselled his love with Helena. At this Gerismond and the rest smiled, and concluded that Montanus and Phoebe should keep their wedding with the two brethren. Aliena seeing Saladyne stand in a dump, to wake him from his dream began thus:

'Why how now, my Saladyne, all amort? what melancholy, man, at the day of marriage? Perchance thou art sorrowful to think on thy brother's high fortunes, and thine own base desires to choose so mean a shepherdess. Cheer up thy heart, man; for this day thou shalt be married to the daughter of a king; for know, Saladyne, I am not Aliena, but Alinda, the daughter of thy mortal enemy Torismond.'

At this all the company was amazed, especially Gerismond, who rising up, took Alinda in his arms, and said to Rosalynde:

'Is this that fair Alinda famous for so many virtues, that forsook her father's court to live with thee exiled in the country?'

'The same,' quoth Rosalynde.

'Then,' quoth Gerismond, turning to Saladyne, 'jolly forester be frolic, for thy fortunes are great, and thy desires excellent; thou hast got a princess as famous for her perfection, as exceeding in proportion.'

'And she hath with her beauty won,' quoth Saladyne, 'an humble servant, as full of faith as she of amiable favour.'

While every one was amazed with these comical events, Corydon came skipping in, and told them that the priest was at church, and tarried for their coming. With that Gerismond led the way, and the rest followed; where to the admiration of all the country swains in Arden their marriages were solemnly solemnized. As soon as the priest had finished home they went with Alinda, where Corydon had made all things in readiness. Dinner was provided, and the tables being spread, and the brides set down by Gerismond, Rosader, Saladyne, and Montanus that day were servitors; homely cheer they had, such as their country could afford, but to mend their fare they had mickle good chat, and many discourses of their loves and fortunes. About mid-dinner, to make them merry, Corydon came in with an old crowd, and played them a fit of mirth, to which he sung this pleasant song:

Corydon's Song

A blithe and bonny country lass,
    heigh ho, the bonny lass!
Sate sighing on the tender grass
    and weeping said, will none come woo her.
A smicker boy, a lither swain,
    heigh ho, a smicker swain!
That in his love was wanton fain,
    with smiling looks straight came unto her.

Whenas the wanton wench espied,
    heigh ho, when she espied!
The means to make herself a bride,
    she simpered smooth like Bonnybell:
The swain, that saw her squint-eyed kind,
    heigh ho, squint-eyed kind!
His arms about her body twined,
    and: 'Fair lass, how fare ye, well?'

The country kit said: 'Well, forsooth,
    heigh ho, well forsooth!
But that I have a longing tooth,
    a longing tooth that makes me cry.'
'Alas!' said he, 'what gars thy grief?
    heigh ho, what gars thy grief?'
'A wound,' quoth she, 'without relief,
    I fear a maid that I shall die.'
'If that be all,' the shepherd said,
    heigh ho, the shepherd said!
'Ile make thee wive it gentle maid,
    and so recure thy malady.'

M

> Hereon they kissed with many an oath,
>   heigh ho, with many an oath!
> And fore God Pan did plight their troth,
>   and to the church they hied them fast.
> And God send every pretty peat,
>   heigh ho, the pretty peat!
> That fears to die of this conceit,
>   so kind a friend to help at last.

Còrydon having thus made them merry, as they were in the midst of their jollity, word was brought in to Saladyne and Rosader that a brother of theirs, one Fernandyne, was arrived, and desired to speak with them. Gerismond overhearing this news, demanded who it was.

'It is, sir,' quoth Rosader, 'our middle brother, that lives a scholar in Paris; but what fortune hath driven him to seek us out I know not.'

With that Saladyne went and met his brother, whom he welcomed with all courtesy, and Rosader gave him no less friendly entertainment; brought he was by his two brothers into the parlour where they all sate at dinner. Fernandyne, as one that knew as many manners as he could points of sophistry, and was as well brought up as well lettered, saluted them all. But when he espied Gerismond, kneeling on his knee he did him what reverence belonged to his estate, and with that burst forth into these speeches:

'Although, right mighty prince, this day of my brother's marriage be a day of mirth, yet time craves another course; and therefore from dainty cates rise to sharp weapons. And you, the sons of Sir John of Bordeaux, leave off your amours and fall to arms; change your loves into lances, and now this day show yourselves as valiant as hitherto you have been passionate. For know, Gerismond, that hard by at the edge of this forest the twelve peers of France are up in arms to recover thy right; and Torismond, trooped with a crew of desperate runagates, is ready to bid them battle. The armies are ready to join; therefore show thyself in the field to encourage thy subjects. And you, Saladyne and Rosader, mount you, and show yourselves as hardy soldiers as you have been hearty lovers; so shall you, for the benefit of your country, discover the idea of your father's virtues to be stamped in your thoughts, and prove children worthy of so honourable a parent.'

At this alarm, given him by Fernandyne, Gerismond leaped from the board, and Saladyne and Rosader betook themselves to their weapons.

'Nay,' quoth Gerismond, 'go with me; I have horse and armour for us all, and then, being well mounted, let us show that we carry revenge and honour at our falchions' points.'

Thus they leave the brides full of sorrow, especially Alinda, who desired Gerismond to be good to her father. He, not returning a word because his haste was great, hied him home to his lodge, where he delivered Saladyne and Rosader horse and armour, and himself armed royally led the way; not having ridden two leagues before they discovered where in a valley both the battles were joined. Gerismond seeing the wing wherein the peers fought, thrust in there, and cried ' Saint Denis! ' Gerismond laying on such load upon his enemies, that he showed how highly he did estimate of a crown. When the peers perceived that their lawful king was there, they grew more eager ; and Saladyne and Rosader so behaved themselves, that none durst stand in their way, nor abide the fury of their weapons. To be short, the peers were conquerors, Torismond's army put to flight, and himself slain in battle. The peers then gathered themselves together, and saluted their king, conducted him royally into Paris, where he was received with great joy of all the citizens. As soon as all was quiet and he had received again the crown, he sent for Alinda and Rosalynde to the court, Alinda being very passionate for the death of her father, yet brooking it with the more patience, in that she was contented with the welfare of her Saladyne.

Well, as soon as they were come to Paris, Gerismond made a royal feast for the peers and lords of his land, which continued thirty days, in which time summoning a parliament, by the consent of his nobles he created Rosader heir apparent to the kingdom ; he restored Saladyne to all his father's land and gave him the Dukedom of Nameurs ; he made Fernandyne principal secretary to himself; and that fortune might every way seem frolic, he made Montanus lord over all the forest of Arden, Adam Spencer Captain of the King's Guard, and Corydon master of Alinda's flocks.

HERE, gentlemen, may you see in Euphues' Golden Legacy, that such as neglect their fathers' precepts, incur much prejudice ; that division in nature, as it is a blemish in nurture, so 'tis a breach of good fortunes ; that virtue is not measured by birth but by action ; that younger brethren, though inferior in years, yet may be superior to honours ; that concord is the sweetest conclusion, and amity betwixt brothers more forceable than fortune.   If you gather any fruits by this Legacy, speak well of Euphues for writing it, and me for fetching it.   If you grace me with that favour, you encourage me to be more forward ; and as soon as I have overlooked my labours, expect the Sailor's Calendar.

T. LODGE.

FINIS

TEXTUAL NOTES

I HAVE recorded in these notes all the variants between the two earliest editions, those namely of 1590 and 1592. The first edition affords a very correct text, and except for the correction of a few obvious misprints, usually retained in the second, there are barely half-a-dozen cases, exclusive of Latin quotations, in which I have departed from its readings. On the other hand there are just a very few alterations in the second edition which suggest that they may be due to the author, and it therefore seemed advisable to give the variations in full. None of the later editions appear to possess independent authority. In a solitary instance where both 1590 and 1592 are corrupt I have inserted a form of a word found in that of 1598 in preference to that now current, but only because it occurs elsewhere in the earlier texts.

P. xxvi, l. 5. *T. L. G.* i.e. Thomas Lodge, Gentleman.

l. 21. *and after falling* 1590 : *and afterwards falling* 1592.

P. xxviii, ll. 10, 11. *Your Honours souldier humbly affectionate* 1590 : *Your honors souldior most humbly affectionate* 1592.

P. xxx. Although an integral part of the composition, without which neither the title-page nor the epilogue (p. 165) is intelligible, this 'Schedule' appears to have been first printed in the edition of 1592.

P. 1, l. 19. *map of age* 1590 : *map of his age* 1592.

P. 3, l. 3. *ingrauen as well the excellence* 1590 : *ingraued as well the excellency* 1592.

l. 21. *that surpasse in blacknesse* 1590 : *that exceed in blacknes* 1592.

l. 23. *stumble vppon stones* 1590 : *stumble vpon the stones* 1592.

P. 4, l. 3. *tenere* 1590 : *tenuere* 1592.

l. 7. *high stretcht* 1590 : *high stretcn* 1592.

l. 23. *is oft hid the most trecherie* 1590 : *is oft hid most trechery* 1592.

l. 26. *let time be touchstone* 1590 : *let time be the touchstone* 1592.

P. 5, l. 2. *that is an extreame* 1590 : *that is extreme* 1592.

l. 13. *deadly desires* 1590 : *deadly destres* 1592.

l. 20. *mine eyes dimme* 1590 : *mine eyes waxeth dimme* 1592.

P. 7, l. 9. *be thy gaine* 1590 : *be your gaine* 1592.

l. 16. *Lillies are faire in shew, but foule in smell.*

It almost looks as though this was the origin of the famous line : ' Lillies that fester, smell far worse then weeds,' in Shakespeare's *Sonnets* (94, l. 14), and in *Edward III*, II. i. 451.

l. 25. *thy . . . thee* 1590 : *your . . . you* 1592.

l. 26. *befriend him thou agen* 1590 : *befriend you him agen* 1592.

l. 28. *from out thy hiue* 1590 : *from out the hiue* 1592.

l. 30. *my sonne* 1590 : *my sonnes* 1592.

P. 8, l. 2. *thy . . . thy* 1590 : *your . . . your* 1592.

l. 17. Horace, *Epist.* i. 10. 24. Both 1590 and 1592 wrongly insert *licet* after *furca*.

l. 18. *So fared it* 1590 : *So fares it* 1592.

P. 9, l. 17. *the carelesse ruine of thy brothers welfare ? why shouldst not thou bee the piller of thy brothers prosperitie* 1590 : *the carelesse ruine of thy brothers prosperitie* 1592.

P. 11, l. 10. *Ah quoth he* 1590 : *As quoth hee* 1592.

P. 21, l. 17. *Troian* 1590–2. This might of course stand for 'Trojan,' but cf. p. 133, l. 24.

P. 23, l. 17. *what they wanted in meate, Rosader supplied with drinke* 1590 : *what they wanted in meat, was supplyed with drinke* 1592.

l. 21. *all tooke their leaues of Rosader* 1590 : *all tooke their leaue of Rosader* 1592.

P. 25, l. 18. *to thinke of loue* 1590 : *to thinke on Loue* 1592.

P. 26, l. 8. *sooner content with a dram of giue me, than a pound of heare me* 1590 : *sooner content with a pound of giue me, than a dram of heare me* 1592.

P. 29 (side note). *in defence of faire Rosalynde* 1590 : *in Defence of Rosalynde* 1592.

P. 31, l. 21. *if he refused to doo, either* 1590 : *if he refused, eyther* 1592.

P. 34, l. 20. *and Alinda (from her royall weedes) put her selfe in more homelie attire. Thus fitted to the purpose, away goe these two friends, hauing now changed their names, Alinda being called Aliena* 1590 : *and Alinda being called Aliena* 1592.

P. 38, l. 1. Before this 1592 inserts another stanza made up of the first two lines of the fourth and the last four of the third.

P. 40, l. 20. *by Phœbes bitter scorne* 1590 : *by Phœbus bitter scorn* 1592.

P. 45, l. 8. *Call home thy flockes in time* 1590 : *Call home thy flocks betime* 1592.

l. 11. *In amore hæc omnia insunt vitia* 1590 : *In amore hæc insunt vitia* 1592.

ll. 11–13. Terence, *Eunuchus*, l. i. 15. The correct reading is :

> In amore haec omnia insunt vitia ; iniuriae,
> Suspitiones, inimicitiae, induciae,
> Bellum, pax rursum.   Incerta haec si tu postules
> Ratione certa facere ; nihilo plus agas,
> Quam si des operam, ut cum ratione insanias.

P. 46, l. 23. *so dangerous a forrest* 1590 : *so dangerous forest* 1592.

P. 47, l. 25. *exceede not in diet* 1590 : *exceed not ill dyet* 1592.

P. 49, l. 1. *Cupid requires* 1590 : *Cupid requireth* 1592.

l. 9. *in her heart* 1590 : *in heart* 1592.

P. 51, l. 27. *Coridon swept a barga[i]ne* 1590 : *Coridon swapt a bargaine* 1592.   The word should most likely be *swapped* or *swopped*, but I am by no means sure that *swept* is an impossible form.

P. 52, l. 13. *surprised his brother beeing a sleepe* 1590 : *surprised his brother when he was a sleepe* 1592.

P. 57, l. 5. *began first to faint* 1590 : *began to faint* 1592.

l. 12. *for a few faire flowers* 1590 : *for a fewe flowers* 1592.

P. 59, l. 7. *he rise vp* 1590 : *he rose vp* 1592.

P. 60, l. 3. *wisht Adam Spencer* 1590 : *wisht A. Spencer* 1592.

l. 24. *to such men as are* 1590 : *to suche as are* 1592.

P. 61, l. 9. *but be Lord of the feast* 1590 : *but the lord of the feast* 1592.

P. 62, l. 2. *discourse, (if it were not* 1590: *discourse, (as it were not* 1592.

P. 63, l. 5. *affections betweene Alinda and her* 1590: *affections betwixt Alinda and her* 1592.

l. 10. *This newes driue the King* 1590–2. Here *drive* may, of course, be a misprint for *drove* (or *drave*, the reading of 1598, which I have substituted in the text), though it is perhaps more likely that Lodge has got confused both as to number and tense. I do not think that *drive* is a possible form of the preterite, the only recorded instance of its use as such being about two centuries earlier.

P. 66, l. 5. *since as the one is knowen* 1590: *since that the one is knowne* 1592.

l. 9. *the barke of a Myrtle tree* 1590: *the bark of a Mir tre* 1592.

P. 70, l. 8. *then doo me that fauour* 1590: *then doo that fauour* 1592.

P. 72, l. 17. *if not as comely, it may be more curteous* 1590: *if not as comely, as courteous* 1592.

P. 73, l. 7. *leaving Aliena and Ganimede to their prittle prattle* 1590: *leauing them to their prittle prattle* 1592.

P. 74, l. 7. *for cutting in by intreats* 1590: *for entring in by intreats* 1593.

P. 78, l. 26. *(quoth Ganimede)* 1590–2. An obvious error for *(quoth Rosader)*.

P. 83, l. 15. *Loue then in euerie flower is found* 1590: *Loue then euery floure is found* 1592.

P. 84, l. 10. *Tis not her frowardnesse* 1590: *Tis neither frowardnesse* 1592.

P. 85, l. 8. *out of this amorous melancholie* 1590: *out of his amorous melancholy* 1592.

P. 86, l. 11. *Or what or thoughts* 1590 : *Or what our thoughts* 1592.

l. 19. *All pale in lookes, and I though young in yeares* 1590–2. Being unable to make any sense of the line as it stands, I have ventured on what seems an obvious emendation (reading *am* for *and*).

P. 88, l. 2. *than anie wooll more softer* 1590 : *that any wooll more softer* 1592.

P. 89, l. 7. *And restlesse horror* 1590 : *And retchless horror* 1592.

P. 90, l. 2. *iumpt I not all vp* 1590 : *iumpe I not all vp* 1592.

P. 94, l. 20. *for either he must resolue* 1590 : *for he must eyther resolue* 1592.

P. 96, l. 2. *and yet the most hardiest* 1590 : *and the most hardiest* 1592.

P. 97, l. 4. *at the sodayne sight of so monstrous a beast lie slaine by him* 1590 : *at the sudden sight of so monstrous a beast lying slaine by him* 1592. The reading of the earlier edition (which being quite impossible I have ventured to alter) was presumably due to a confusion of construction.

P. 98, l. 3. *I counted it the hart of a resolute man* 1590 : *I counted it the part of a resolute man* 1592. I am a little doubtful whether the earlier reading is actually a misprint, but the later gives such obviously better sense that I have adopted it.

l. 8. *thy present fortunes* 1590 : *thy present misfortunes* 1592.

P. 99, l. 17. *teares from mine eyes* 1590 : *tears from my eyes* 1592.

P. 102, l. 17. *thus should it be* 1590 : *thus it should be* 1592.

P. 103, l. 14. *hauing Loue in her heart* 1590 : *hauing Loue in heart* 1592.

P. 105, l. 12. *were in this sad talk* 1590: *were in sad talke* 1592.

P. 106, l. 20. *relieue our fortunes, as we holde you valiant, so we esteeme you courteous, and to haue* 1590: *relieue our fortunes, & to haue* 1592.

P. 110, l. 9. *might be subjects to fancie* 1590: *might be subject to fancy* 1592.

l. 19. *but for all these vertues* 1590: *and for all these vertues* 1592.

P. 112, l. 21. *that like loue in no shape* 1590: *that like Ioue in no shape* 1592.

P. 113, ll. 7–11. Horace, *Satires*, ii. 3, 94. 1590 and 1592 read wrongly: ' quas qui constrinxerit ille Clarus erit, fortis, iustus, sapiens, etiam & rex.'

P. 114, l. 16. *the foldes of my fare* 1590: *the foldes of my face* 1592. The earlier reading can hardly be anything but a misprint.

P. 115, l. 11. *you and Ganimede but to walke* 1590: *you and Ganimede to walke* 1592.

P. 119, l. 1. *Which made the Gods forsake* 1590: *Which make the Gods forsake* 1592.

l. 16. *thou regardest not my maladie* 1590: *thou regardest not thy maladie* 1592.

P. 120, l. 4. *my face may decypher the sorrowes* 1590: *my face may discouer the sorrows* 1592.

P. 121, l. 6. *your market may be made* 1590: *your market can be made* 1592.

l. 15. *thou shalt liue by losse* 1590: *thou shalt but liue by losse* 1592.

P. 124, l. 15. *your selues can desire, or I imagine* 1590: *your selues can desire, or imagine* 1592.

P. 125, l. 2. *that our mishap might salue his maladie* 1590: *that your mishap might salue his malady* 1592.

P. 126, l. 4. *discouer her secrete aphorismes* 1590 : *discouer our secret aphorismes* 1592.

P. 128, ll. 3–4. Ovid, *Remedia Amoris*, 139–40.

P. 130, l. 3. *words as preiudiciall as the charmes of Circes* 1590 : *words are preiudiciall as the charmes of Circes* 1592.

l. 14. *pearch with the Kistresse* 1590-2. No doubt a misprint for *kistrelle* or *kestrel,* no such form as that in the old editions being otherwise recorded.

P. 136, l. 6. *I loue thee at the first looke* 1590 : *I loued thee at the first looke* 1592.

P. 140, l. 15. Both 1590 and 1592 misprint *Bellephoron* for *Bellerophon.*

P. 141, l. 18. *of so deepe a distresse* 1590 : *of so deepe distresse* 1592.

l. 20. *entangled her affection* 1590 : *intangled her affections* 1592.

l. 23. *beautie to content thine eye* 1590 : *beauty to please thine eye* 1592.

P. 142, l. 27. *I will home by our house* 1590-2. Possibly 1598 is right in reading *to our house.*

P. 143, l. 21. *and wresteth the wealth of nature* 1590 : *and wrests the wealth of nature* 1592.

P. 144, l. 22. *Festina Lente* 1590 : *Festina Lenter* 1592.

l. 23. *fancies are oft times the fruites* 1590 : *fancies are oftentimes the fruits* 1592.

P. 145, l. 23. *frowardnesse toward the Shepheard* 1590 : *frowardnesse towards the shepheard* 1592.

P. 146, l. 14. *tooke his leaue of his Phœbe* 1590 : *tooke his leaue of Phœbe* 1592.

P. 148, l. 14. *wanting to this marriage* 1590 : *wanting to his marriage* 1592.

P. 151, l. 23. *sucking their full* 1590 : *sucking their fill* 1592.

P. 152, l. 3, *for being so mean,* to p. 161, l. 27, *heigh ho the shepheard said.* Sheet R is wanting in the only known copy of 1590. For this portion, therefore, we have to rely on 1592 alone.

P. 155, l. 13. *Loue (sir) is charitie in his lawes* 1590–2. I have no doubt that *charitie* is a corruption (perhaps for some legal term), but I cannot see that Collier's suggestion *charie* helps matters.

P. 161. Corydon's Song is imitated from Spenser's 'Bonnybell' ballad in the *Shepherd's Calendar* (viii. ll. 53, etc.) which explains the name in l. 13. The old editions print four eight-line stanzas and a quatrain. I have made the third stanza consist of twelve lines and the fourth of eight, on account of the rimes.

l. 5. *and weeping said, will none come woo me ?* 1592. I have ventured to alter *me* to *her* in order to restore the rime. The direct has evidently been somehow substituted for the indirect question. Possibly we should also read *would* for *will.*

P. 162, ll. 1–2. *a oath* 1590–2. This I have ventured to alter.

ll. 3–4. This extraordinary mixture of mythologies is also borrowed from Spenser, who supplied a notable example in the line : 'She raignes a goddesse now emong the saintes' (*Shep. Cal.* xi. 175).

P. 163, l. 4. *shew your selues as valiant, as hethertoo you haue been passionate* 1590 : *shew your selues valiant, as hitherto you haue been passionate* 1592.

P. 164, l. 3. *cried Saint Denis, Gerismond laying on* 1590 : *cryed S. Denis, laying on* 1592.

P. 165, l. 13. *T. Lodge* 1590 : *Th. Lodge* 1592.

GLOSSARIAL INDEX

Note.—The words in this glossary fall into three groups: (i) common Elizabethan words and forms which may be unfamiliar to modern readers; (ii) rare words, forms and uses for which illustrative quotations are often desired; (iii) words and names belonging to the Euphuistic vocabulary, and also proverbial phrases, to which references are useful. I have indexed the second group rather carefully since the vagueness of the references given makes me suspect that *Rosalynde* was not read for the *New English Dictionary*.

ARDEN, Ardennes, 16, 31, 56, etc.
AREDE, advice, 41
ARGUS, 130
ATTAINT, touch, 36
AUGURISM, augury, 92
AUTHENTICAL, authoritative, 10, 128
AVICEN, 9
AWAKE, waking, 97

BAARAN LEAF, 4
BAIN, bathe, 79, 83
BALE, evil, 25
BALEFUL, evil, 25
BALSAMUM, balm, 96
BASH, be abashed, 101
BAVIN, faggot, 6
BECOME, suit (of a person), 34
BEE, 129
BELLEROPHON, 140
BEWRAY, reveal, 2, etc.
BEZO LES LABRES, salutation (I kiss your lips), 15
BIARES, presumably an error for Briareus, 6
BIRD, 'one bird in the hand is worth two in the wood,' 78
BLACK OX, misfortune (in proverbial phrase), 34

BLENDED, dazzled, deluded, 118
BLOOMS, blossoms, 58
BLUBBERED, spoke weeping, 145
BONNET, cap, 48, 149
BOWSE, drink deeply (the same as 'booze'), 130
BOWSETH, in the sense of bathes or dips. Probably an unusual, or erroneous, application of the word, current as a hawking term with the meaning of drinking frequently and much. It may however have some relation to the word 'bowssen,' to duck, from Cornish 'beuzi,' to immerse, drown, 79
BRIGHT, brightness, 37
BRUITED, noised, rumoured, 134
BUNCH, pack of cards, 12
BUTTERY, store-room, properly for liquor, 23

CAMILLA, wife of Philautus in *Euphues* (q. v.), xxx
CARBUNCLE, 99, 114
CAREW (or more correctly Carey), Edmund and

Fop, foolish person, 111

Force, 'of force,' necessarily, xxvii

Forefinger kiss, blown kiss, 126

Forthy, therefore, 41

Fortune (her emblem), 57

Frame, manner, 42

Free (horse), noble (?), 15

Friends, befriends, 7

Front, forehead, 133

Froward, untoward, 49, etc.

Funerals, funeral rites, 6

Galatea (and Polyphemus, see Theocritus, Idyl vi), 116

Galen, 10

Gars, causes, 161

Gat, got, 15

Giglot, loose woman, 109

Give, 'my mind gives me,' inform, 60

Gladded, gladdened, 48

Glance at, make fun of, tease, 138

Glide, course, 37

Greet, weep, 40

Halcyones, birds, 3

Halfpenny, 'your heart on your halfpenny,' to have a particular object in view, 12

Hamper, entangle, constrain, 107

Handselled, sealed, concluded, inaugurated, 159

Handy, manual, 112

Hap, fortune, 42

Happily, perhaps, 103

Haste, 'he is in haste whom the devil drives,' 75

Herehault, herald, 63

Hery, praise, 41, 43

Hobby, a species of small falcon (xxvii), 3, 139

Hoby (or Hobby), Sir Edward, son of Sir Thomas, the translator of the *Cortegiano*, xxvii

Humour, disposition, 9

Hunsdon, Lord of, Henry Carey, first Baron Hunsdon in 1559, Lord Chamberlain since 1583, and later patron of the company of actors which included Shakespeare. He does not seem to have been Governor of Berwick after 1587, xxvi

Hyena, 8

HYPERBOREI, 4, 128, 144

IMPERIAL (sometimes written 'emperial'), the meaning influenced in this, as in many other cases, by the resemblance with 'empyreal,' empyrean, 70

IMPLAISTER, plaster, 32

INEQUAL, unequal, 56

INFER, support the inference of, 131

INFORTUNATE, unfortunate, 24, 136

INGRATEFUL, ungrateful, 98, 107

INTERPARLEYS, conferences, conversation, 84

JEALOUS, suspicious, 126

JEOPARDY, uncertainty, danger, 40

JET (sb.), 76, 131

JETS, struts, 109

JUMPED, concluded, 90

KERSEY, coarse cloth, 149

KESTREL, a species of hawk, 130

KIND, nature, natural faculty or power, 138

KIT, kitten, girl, 161

LACHET, thong, xxix

LANDSLORD, landlord, 47, 48, 51

LATMOS, 16

LEAVELESS, leafless, 116

LEPANTHUS, shores of, 4

LETTUCE FOR YOUR LIPS, suitable for you, 121

LEVELLING OUT, discovering, revealing, 128

LIEU, 'in lieu of,' in return for, 140

LIMON, lemon (the former being the more etymological form), 39, 60, 108

LION, 8

LIQUORICE LEAF, 4

LIST, will, liking, 129

LITHER, nimble, 161

LOAD, 'lay a load on,' beat, 13, 106, 164

LOCKRAM, linen, 149

LODESTAR, guiding star, polestar, 3, 73

LOSELS, worthless fellows, 56

LUNA, 16

LUNISEQUA (star), 83

LUPUS EST IN FABULA, an expression signifying 'a person we are talking of, or one concerned, is present,' 104

MAKE, mate, 119

MALGRADO, in spite of, 142

MARKET IS MARRED, 142

MAZE, possibly, though not, I think, probably, an error or confusion or wilful perversion for 'muse,' a technical term for the opening in a thicket through which a hare habitually passes (the corresponding term for a deer is 'entry'). If we suppose that 'muse' is meant, a punning allusion to the 'perplexed' of the previous line is obvious, 123

MAZER, wooden cup, 91, 108, 150

MEMENTO, musing, 19, 20, 77

MERCILESS, unpardonable, 59

MIRRAH, for myrrh-tree, 36

MOLE, stain, 82

MOMUS, xxix

MORROW, morning, 15

MOURN, mourning, 87

NARCISSUS, 51

NECK, formerly a man carried a weapon on his 'neck,' whereas now he carries it on his 'shoulder,' 95, 103, 106, etc.

NEGROMANCY, necromancy (the spelling indicates a false etymology — from *niger* instead of νεκρός — which has undoubtedly affected the connotation of the word), 147

NOSE (bleeding), 94

NOURITURE, nurture, upbringing, 30

ON, of, 113

ON SLEEP, asleep, 112

ORIENT, oriental, hence precious, excellent, 33, 69; (of a flower) springing, blooming (?), 41

OUGHT, owed, 53

OVER-READ, re-read, 138

OWN, 'the own,' its own, 'a foul bird defiles the own nest,' 37; (i.e. belonging to the slop), 149

PAD, toad, the phrase 'a pad in the straw,' meaning a hidden danger, was proverbial, 14

PALM TREE, 2, 58

PANTHER, 76

ROVE, to shoot at rovers, that is casual marks, not at a fixed distance, hence to shoot wildly at long range, 139

RUNAGATES, vagabonds, 163

SAILORS' CALENDAR, a book by Lodge, not now known, 165

SAINT DENIS!—war-cry of the French kings, 164

SATE, sat, 18, 46, 48, etc.

SCORPION, 140

SECRETARY, confidant, 134

SENDAL, a light silk, 148, 158

SET UP HER REST, fix her abode, 51

SETHIN LEAF, 5

SHADOW, hide, cover, 22

SHOWED, shown, 59

SICCO PEDE, (dry-foot) carelessly, 53

SINOPLE TREE, 125

SITH, since, 58, 154

SLOP, loose breeches, 149

SMICKER, smart, 161

SOUSETH, swoopeth (hawking term), 69

SPATTANA (herb), 144

SPRIGHT, spirit, 127

SQUINT-EYED, indirect, 161

STANDISH, ink-stand, 135

START, started, 35

STICKLER, arbitrator, manager, 149

STOCK, stocking, 149

STRICKEN UP, struck, concluded (of a bargain), 91

STROKE, struck, 95

SUBMISS, submissive, 101

SWAN, 2

SWEPT (or swapt?), concluded (a bargain), 51

TAINT, dye, stain, colour, 16, etc.

TALL, bold, 55

TANAIS, 35

TARANTULA, 152

TEINTURE, dye, 133, 155

TELLUS, the earth, 39

TENERIFA, Tenerif, 130

TERCERAS, presumably Terceira in the Azores, xxvii, xxix

THRALL, bondage, 147

TIGER, 8

TOPAS, 113

TRACT (sb.), track, 39; (vb.) trace, 44

TRAINS, plots, devices, 41

TROOPED, followed, 163

TROTH, faith, truth, 48, 126

TROYAN, Trojan, 21 (*see* note), 133

TRUNCHEON, spear, 140

TRUSSED, packed, 34

TYRE, apparently used for Carthage, as being a Phoenician colony, 81

UNCAPABLE, incapable, 42

UNPERFECT, imperfect, 72, 95

UPSEE FREEZE, toast, carouse, 23

VAILED, doffed, removed, 15, 19

VENY, assault, 107

WANTON . . . WANT ONE (the supposed etymology), 5, 80

WASP, 130

WATER PLANTS, weep, 144

WATERCRESSES, 145

WEED, garment, 37

WELTED, edged, 149

WHAT, why, 114

WHERE, whereas, 4

WHILE, until, 54, 111

WHIPPED, gathered, sewn over, 149

WIND (vb.), blow, 86; (sb.) 'is the wind in that door,' is that what is the matter, 112

WIVE IT, become a wife, 161

WOLVES OF SYRIA, 139

WORM - SEED, probably by confusion for 'wormwood,' 152

WORSHIPS, honours, 58

WRASTLING, wrestling, 14, 17

WRESTS, wrestles, 136

WRINGS, hurts, 145

WRIT, wrote, x

WRUNG, hurt, 110

ZEUXIS, a Greek painter, 90

APPENDIX

SHAKSPERE'S *AS YOU LIKE IT* AND LODGE'S *ROSALYNDE* COMPARED.[1]

BY W. G. STONE, ESQ.

I PROPOSE in the following paper to examine Shakspere's treatment of Lodge's *Rosalynde*, the source of *As You Like It*, from a negative point of view; and, instead of showing his agreement therewith, to dwell upon his divergence therefrom, (I) in varying the plot, (II) in modifying the characters.

Before considering Shakspere's use of his acknowledged original—Lodge's *Rosalynde*—it may be well to enquire whether he had any other before him. Farmer, who opposed the assertion of Grey and Upton that Shakspere borrowed *As You Like It* from the pseudo-Chaucerian *Tale of Gamelyn*,—to which Lodge was partially indebted,—went so far as to say : ". . . the old bard, who was no hunter of MSS., contented himself solely with Lodge's *Rosalynd*." [2] Knight [3] produced three passages from *Gamelyn*, for which he found parallelisms in *As You Like It*. Orlando was dependent upon his brother's generosity. So should Gamelyn have been

---

[1] A Paper read at the 77th Meeting of the New Shakspere Society, Friday, March 10, 1882 ; reprinted from the *Transactions* of the Society, 1880–6, pp. 277–93.

[2] "On the learning of Shakspeare," in the *Var. Sh.*, 1821, i. 314.

[3] *Pictorial Shakspere*, ed. 1, Comedies, vol. ii. pp. 199–201.

187

if Sire Johan of Boundys had followed the advice of some "wise knightes" whom he had requested to divide his lands between his three sons, having special regard to his youngest son's, Gamelyn's, interest.

"For to delen hem alle to oon, that was her thought,
And for Gamelyn was yongest, he schuld have nought"
(ll. 43, 44).[1]

Sire Johan, however, made Gamelyn his residuary legatee. In the next instance there is certainly an analogous treatment of subject. The old man, whose sons had been well nigh slain by Charles, was "making such pittiful dole ouer them, that all the beholders take his part with weeping," said Le Beau (I. ii. 139, 140). When Gamelyn reached the wrestling-place :

". . . he herd a frankeleyn wayloway synge,
And bigan bitterly his hondes for to wrynge" (ll. 197, 198),

bemoaning the death of his two sons. Contrast the stoicism of Lodge's franklin who "never chaunged his countenance, but as a man of a couragious resolution, tooke up the bodies of his sonnes without shewe of outward discontent." The people, we are told, "murmured, and were all in a deepe passion of pittie"[2] (p. 18). The "shake by the shoulder," wherewith Lodge's wrestler disturbs Rosader's contemplation of

[1] The references are to the Aldine edition of *Chaucer* (ed. 2), vol. ii. pp. 139 *et sqq.* The Rev. W. A. Harrison drew my attention to the parallelisms in *Gamelyn* at ll. 71-73 ; 193, 194 ; and 233, 234. [A critical text of *Gamelyn*, edited by Professor Skeat, has since been published by the Clarendon Press, separately and in the six-volume edition of Chaucer.]

[2] The references to *Rosalynde*, which were originally to the reprint in Hazlitt's *Sh. Lib.*, have been made to agree with the present edition, but the old spelling has been retained.

Rosalynd's charms (p. 19), bears I think, a closer resemblance to Charles's rude interruption of Orlando's talk with Rosalind and Celia,—" Come, where is this yong gallant that is so desirous to lie with his mother earth " (I. ii. 212, 213),—than can be found in the taunt addressed by the champion to Gamelyn:

> ". . . Who is thy fader and who is thy sire?
> For-sothe thou art a gret fool, that thou come hire "
> (ll. 221, 222).

Five other parallelisms, more or less clear, may be added. After his father's death, Johan, Gamelyn's eldest brother,

> ". . . took into his hond his lond and his leede,
> And Gamelyn himselfe to clothen and to feede.
> He clothed him and *fed him yvel* and eek wrothe "
> (ll. 71–73).

Orlando complains to Adam that Oliver's " horses are bred better, for besides that they are faire with their *feeding*, they are taught their mannage, . . . hee lets mee *feede* with his Hindes, barres mee the place of a brother," &c. (I. i. 11–13, 19–21). Lodge only says, generally, that Saladyne made " Rosader his foote boy for the space of two or three yeares, keeping him in such servile subjection, as if he had been the sonne of any country vassal " (p. 10–11). When Oliver called Orlando a " villaine," the latter replied: " I am no villaine: I am the yongest sonne of Sir Rowland de Boys; he was my father; and he is thrice a villaine that saies such a father begot villaines " (I. i. 59–62). Gamelyn answered the epithet " gadelyng," given him by his eldest brother, Johan, thus:

> " I am no worse gadelyng, ne no worse wight,
> But born of a lady, and geten of a knight " (ll. 107, 108).

As Gamelyn rode away to the wrestling-match, Johan

". . . bysoughte Jhesu Crist, that is heven kyng,
He mighte *breke his nekke* in that wrastlyng" (ll. 193, 194).

In commending Orlando to Charles's "discretion," Oliver
said: "I had as liefe thou didst *breake his necke* as his finger"
(I. i. 152, 153). The wrestler thus taunted Gamelyn (ll.
233, 234):

" ' By God ! ' sayde the champioun, ' welcome mote thou be !
Come thou ones in myn hond, schalt thou never the
[thrive].' "

Duke Frederick said: "You shall trie but one fall."
Charles answered: "No, I warrant your Grace, you shall
not entreat him to a second,"[1] &c. (I. ii. 216–218).

[1] While on this subject of the wrestling as treated by Chaucer and by
Shakspere, I would point to a coincidence which seems to me to
throw some light on a disputed reading of a passage in *As You Like It*
(II. iii. 7, 8).

"Why would you be so fond to ouercome
The *bonnie* [? *bonie*] *priser* of the humorous Duke?"

says Adam to Orlando. The modern texts read " Bonny prizer";
"bonny" being taken in the sense of the Scotch "bonnie," as in the
expression "a bonnie lass." The epithet is suitable enough when
applied to a fair damsel, but is it applicable to a man? I do not
believe that Shakspere would be likely to use it of Charles in any
case ; and certainly he would not put it into the mouth of Adam under
the circumstances in which he is speaking. The word occurs in
Henry VI., part 2 (V. ii. 12), where it is applied to a fine horse, "the
bonnie beast he loved so well." In the *Taming of the Shrew* (II. i. 186),
where "Bonny Kate" is given in the Folio as "BONY Kate." In
the same play (III. ii. 226), where it is "bonny Kate." In *Richard III.*
(I. i. 94), where Shore's wife is said to have "a bonny eye." In the
Song in *Much Ado about Nothing* (II. iii. 68), "blithe and bonnie."

Lastly, the forest of Arden and that to which Gamelyn and Adam the spencer—the prototype of old Adam—betook themselves are described by the same adjective. Adam remarked :

> " That lever me were keyes for to bere,
> Then walken in this *wilde woode* my clothes to tere "
> (ll. 621, 622).

Compare :

> " And to the skirts of this *wilde Wood* he [Duke Frederick] came (V. iv. 165).

Prizer (it is spelled " priser " in the Folio) is explained to mean one who fights for prizes—prize-fighter. I strongly suspect that both these derivations are wrong ; that (a) " Bonnie " should be " bony," as Dyce and others have printed the word in their editions, meaning one with large bones, and so with a strong powerful frame ; and (b) that "priser" means one who lays hold with a good firm grip. Cotgrave has the word in this sense, " *estre en prises,* to be closely locked or grappled together ; to tug one another ; to *wrastle* or strive with one another."

So that the expressions taken together would mean *the big-framed wrestler.*

Aldis Wright objects to " Bony," that it would describe a thin and skeleton-like man. But then he takes PRIZER = prize-fighter ; and the question is whether Bony taken with " PRISER " would not convey the idea of a man whose big bones gave him the advantage in the grip.

Bearing in mind that Shakspere has, in the preceding scene, described his wrestler as " *the sinewy Charles,*" now hear what Chaucer says of a wrestler :

> " The Mellere was a stout carle for the nones,
> Full big he was of *braun,* and *eke* of *boones ;*
> That prevede wel, for overal ther he cam,
> At wrastlynge he wolde bere awey the ram."
> (*Prologue,* ll. 545–548.)—W. A. Harrison.

I. Variations in the Plot.

1. We meet with a slight variation in the opening scene of *As You Like It*. Sir John of Bordeaux (Sir Rowland de Boys) bequeathed to his youngest son Rosader (Orlando) a larger portion than either Saladyne or Fernandyne (Oliver and Jaques de Boys) received. Rosader was thus no penniless younger brother like Orlando, but, being a minor at the time of Sir John's death, he was left to the guardianship of Saladyne, who wasted his estates and degraded him to the condition of a foot-boy (pp. 8–11).

2. When the two brothers quarrelled, Saladyne bade his men bind Rosader, who thereupon caught up a rake and used it so vigorously as to put them all to flight, and compel Saladyne to take refuge in a loft (p. 13). This brawl is reduced by Shakspere to Orlando's momentary clutch of Oliver's throat (I. i. 62–64).

3. After his victory in the wrestling-match, Rosader, attended by some "boon companions," returned triumphantly to Saladyne's house. Saladyne had bribed the wrestler to kill his brother, and, being wroth at the failure of his scheme, shut the gate against them. Rosader broke open the gate and welcomed his comrades to five tuns of Saladynes's wine and whatever food could be found. When the guests had departed he was minded to avenge Saladyne's discourtesy, but, through Adam Spencer's mediation, the brothers were reconciled. A "long while," we learn, then elapsed till, "on a morning very early," Saladyne surprised Rosader asleep, and caused him to be bound to a post in the hall, forbidding any one to give him food or drink. He was released by Adam Spencer, with whose assistance he attacked Saladyne

and the " kindred and allyes," who were being entertained at
"a solempne breakefast," slew some of them and drove the rest
out of the house. Saladyne returned, accompanied by the
sheriff and twenty-five "tall men." Rosader and Adam
Spencer sallied forth, repulsed the sheriff's forces, and escaped
to the forest of Arden (pp. 22–24, 52–56). All this
violence Shakspere omitted, and made Oliver's meditated
attempt on Orlando's life a reason for the latter's flight
(II. iii. 19–25).

4. Shakspere invented the old enmity between Duke
Frederick and Sir Rowland de Boys, which caused the
duke's ungenerous behaviour to Orlando (I. ii. 237–239).

I here note that the characters and incidents of Shakspere's
original hitherto mentioned were borrowed by Lodge, with
slight alteration, from the *Tale of Gamelyn*. The unnamed
"woode," to which Gamelyn and Adam the spencer
retreated (l. 617), was defined by Lodge as the forest of
Arden (p. 56). The characters added by Lodge and
utilized by Shakspere are: Rosalynd, Alinda (Celia),
Phœbe, Montanus[1] (Silvius), Coridon (Corin), Gerismond,
the banished king (Duke Senior), and Torismond, King of
France (Duke Frederick).

5. Torismond, enraged at Alinda's importunate pleading
for Rosalynd, banished both daughter and niece (p. 31).
There was, as we have seen, a long interval between

---

[1] Shakspere, in changing the names of some of Lodge's characters,
has done so with wonderful propriety, having regard to the scene of the
story. Saladyne becomes Oliver, an appropriate name, from *Olivier*, an
Olive-tree. Sir John of Bordeaux becomes Sir Rowland *de Bois* = Wood.
Montanus is changed to Silvius, one born in the woods; "in silvis
natus" (Livy, I. 3).—W. A. H.

Rosader's triumph and his flight, during which time Rosalynd and Alinda, whose banishment took place on the day of the wrestling-match (cf. pp. 24 and 28), were living in Arden (p. 52). They were known as Aliena and Ganimede, and passed as mistress and page (p. 34). This variation in time lead to these results.

a. When Rosalynd and Alinda had been travelling for two or three days through the "Forrest side," the former espied a posy addressed to an obdurate fair one, and carved on the bark of a pine. Some more verses, signed "Montanus," were discovered by Alinda on a beech (pp. 35–37). In Shakspere's version, Orlando, not an uninteresting shepherd, was the writer of the verses which cast Rosalind into such a pretty flutter of hope and bashfulness.

β. At the banquet in the forest (II. vii.) Gerismond learnt from Rosader how his daughter and niece had been banished, and were gone none knew whither (p. 63). Orlando, whose flight was coeval with Rosalind's, had not this clue for detecting her disguise. Yet I agree with Mr. Grant White[1] that we must allow much for the glamour of Arden forest.

6. Saladyne was imprisoned by Torismond, ostensibly on account of Rosader's wrongs. Being released and exiled he resolved to seek Rosader. He did not recognize his brother in the forester who saved him from a lion, but made known to Rosader, as to a stranger, his previous history and contrition for his misdeeds. Rosader thereupon revealed himself (pp. 63–65, 93–101). Doubtless Oliver knew Orlando when, as he said:

"From miserable slumber I awaked"(IV. iii. 133).

---

[1] *Galaxy*, April, 1875, No. iv, p. 556, col. 1.

7. Two or three[1] days were spent by Rosader in showing his forest haunts to Saladyne, during which time Rosalynd sorely missed her lover (pp. 103–104), to whom, at their last meeting, she had been sportively married by Alinda (p. 90). Rosader then revisited Rosalynd and Alinda, and told them the cause of his absence (p. 104). Oliver informed Rosalind and Celia that Orlando was detained by the wound which he had received from the lioness (IV. iii. 151–157).

8. In the course of this interview "certain Rascals," who were hiding from justice in the forest, endeavoured to carry off Alinda. They overpowered and severely wounded Rosader, and must have succeeded in their attempt had not Saladyne fortunately come to the rescue (pp. 105–106). Shakspere made no use of this adventure.

9. On the next day, when Rosalynd and Alinda had returned to their home, after witnessing Montanus's bootless courtship of Phœbe, came Saladyne, bringing news of Rosader's anticipated restoration to health (pp. 124–125). Rosalynd having discreetly withdrawn (p. 128), Saladyne wooed Alinda and prevailed on her to promise that she would either marry him or "still live a virgine" (p. 132). Shakspere, who omitted the rescue from the ruffians, caused Orlando to be slightly wounded in saving Oliver from the lioness (IV. iii. 147, 148).

10. At an indefinite later date Montanus brought Phœbe's letter to Rosalynd. Silvius delivered a similar missive just before Oliver entered with news of Orlando.

11. A day being fixed for the marriage of Alinda and Saladyne, the feigned Ganimede promised Rosader that, by the aid of a friend "deeply experienst in Necromancy and

---

[1] P. 103. Three days, p. 104.

Magicke," the presence of Rosalynd at the ceremony should be ensured. Hereupon " Rosader frownd, thinking that Ganimede had jested with him " (p. 147). Shakspere made Rosalind herself the conjurer, and inspired Orlando with a vague confidence in the art which she professed to have learnt from her uncle the magician (V. ii. 56–75 ; iv. 3, 4).

12. Gerismond's investigation of the case of Montanus and Phœbe was the chief incident of the wedding festivities (pp. 151–156). Rosalynd and Rosader were left quite in the shade. Shakspere kept his under-plot within due proportions, and imparted breadth and diversity to the closing scene of *As You Like It*, by means of Touchstone's wit.

13. The marriage banquet was interrupted by the arrival of Fernandyne, who announced that the twelve peers of France had taken up arms on their lawful sovereign's behalf, and were about to join battle with Torismond's forces, on the outskirts of the forest. Gerismond, accompanied by Rosader and Saladyne, armed and hastened to the fray, in which Torismond was slain and his followers were routed. Gerismond then returned to Paris in triumph, and the personages of the story received their several rewards, from Rosader downwards, created heir apparent, to Coridon, who became master of Alinda's flocks (pp. 162–164). The repentance of Duke Frederick forestalled the pending hurly-burly (V. iv. 160–171). The "happie number" grouped round the Elder Duke, whose "returned fortune" they are soon to share, are visible to us only while we stand within the enchanted circle of Arden forest.

II. Variations in the Characters.

I turn now to the like negative comparison of the characters presented by the novel and the play.

1. In her meditations, after the wrestling-match, upon her sudden passion for Rosader, Rosalynd lamented falling in love with a poor man who could not maintain her state or revenge her father's wrongs, called to mind certain prudential maxims, as "that gold is sweeter than eloquence; that love is a fire and wealth is the fewel," and exhorted herself to think Rosader "lesse beautiful, because hee is in want, and account his vertues but qualities of course, for that he is not indued with wealth." She ended her soliloquy, however, by abjuring "such servile conceites, as to prize gold more than honor, or to measure a Gentleman by his wealth, not by his vertues" (pp. 26–27). I suspect that Lodge deemed it incumbent on him, as a man of the world, to correct the excessive saccharinity of his love-passages with some bitter infusions of worldly wisdom. In contrast to these musings— whether natural or factitious—we have the momentary struggle with conventional reserve which made Shakspere's Rosalind murmur to herself, when she saw Orlando's wistful gaze fixed on her,

"He cals vs back : my pride fell with my fortunes ;
        Ile aske him what he would " (I. ii. 264, 265).

The Rosalind of the novel is a colourless being, incapable of entering into the spirit of her part, and availing herself of it to tease Rosader with the saucy bewildering banter which Orlando had to endure. The only gleam of merriment in their wooing came when, after they had sung a wooing eclogue together, Rosalynd said : "How now, Forrester, have I not fitted your turne? have I not playde the woman handsomely, and shewed myselfe as coy in graunts, as courteous in desires, and beene as full of suspition, as men of flattery? and yet to salve all, jumpe I not all up with the sweet union of love? Did not Rosalinde content her Rosader?" Rosader opined that "if my foode bee no better than such amorous dreames, Venus at the yeares end shal find me but a leane lover " (pp. 89–90). Of their usual dialogue the following is a fair specimen. "Thou speakest by experience (quoth Ganimede), and therfore we hold al thy words for Axiomes : but is Love such a lingring maladie? It is (quoth he) either extreame or meane, according to the minde of the partie that entertaines it ; for as the weedes grow longer un-toucht then the prettie floures, and the flint lyes safe in the quarry, when the Emerauld is suffering the Lapidaries toole : so meane men are freed from Venus injuries, when kings are environed with a laborinth of her cares " (p. 82).

Whatever capacity for fun was possessed by Lodge's Rosalynd showed itself in her talks with Alinda. Of this I give an example. "You may see (quoth Ginimede) what mad cattel you women be, whose harts sometimes are made of Adamant that wil touch with no impression, and sometimes of wax that is fit for every forme : they delight to be courted, and then they glory to seeme coy, and when they are most desired then they freese with disdaine : and this fault is so common to the sex, that you see it painted out in the shepheardes [Montanus's] passions, who found his Mistres as froward as he was enamoured" (p. 36).

Either in jest or for the sake of proving his constancy she advised Rosader to make his court to Alinda, who had uttered a hope of finding "as faithfull a Paris" as he was (p. 79). Neither motive could, I think, have induced Shakspere's Rosalind to give such counsel to her lover.

When Rosader reappeared, after breaking his tryst, it was Alinda, not Rosalynd, who scolded him. Rosader had been absent for three days (p. 104). Sharp were the reproofs which fell on Orlando, who came "within an houre" of the time appointed (IV. i. 38–52). At first, his offended mistress ignored his presence, and continued—as Grant White [1] has explained to us—to banter the retreating Jaques.

Moreover, Phœbe's cruelty did not move Lodge's Rosalynd to utter severer censures than were these. "And if, Damzell, you fled from mee,"—Phœbe had told Montanus (p. 121) that if he pursued her with Phœbus, she must flee with Daphne,—"I would transforme you as Daphne to a bay, and then in contempt trample your branches under my feet. . . Because thou art beautifull be not so coy : as there is nothing more fair, so there is nothing more fading ; as momentary as the shadowes which growes from a clowdy Sunne" (p. 122). Throughout the speech Phœbe's beauty is fully acknowledged. Contrast with this gentle language the bitter taunts of the Shaksperian Rosalind, and the disparaging epithets which she applied to the poor shepherdess's rustic comeliness : "inkie browes," "black silke haire," "bugle eye-balls," and "cheeke of creame" (III. v. 46, 47). The climax of injury was reached when Silvius brought Phœbe's letter to Rosalind, who, indulging in malicious play upon the double sense of the word "hand," sneered at the "leatherne," "freestone-coloured," "huswiues," hand of the writer ; adding with surpassing scorn,

[1] *Galaxy*, April, 1875, No. iv, p. 556, col. 2.

as though such a defect was, in Phœbe's case, part of the order of Nature, "but that's no matter" [1] (IV. iii. 24–27). Lodge's Rosalynd "fell into a great laughter" on reading the letter, but no gibes followed at the expense of writer or bearer; she merely advised Montanus to transfer his affections to some less hard-hearted fair one (pp. 138–142).

2. Concerning Alinda there is little to be said. Like Celia, she bravely asserted before her father the innocence of the friend whose exile she declared her resolve of sharing. Shakspere omitted this extravagant expression of trust in her friend's loyalty. " If then, Fortune, who tryumphs in varietie of miseries, hath presented some envious person (as minister of her intended stratageme) to tainte Rosalynde with any surmise of treason, let him be brought to her face, and confirme his accusation by witnesses ; which proved, let her die, and Alinda will execute the massacre" (p. 30). Through her position of mistress, and from the absence of any special force of character in Rosalynd, Alinda took the lead of her page.

3. A comparison of Rosader and Orlando elicits several important differences of conception : the advantage decidedly remaining with Shakspere's hero.

Orlando was unable to say even an "I thank you," in response to Rosalind's gracious gift and words (I. ii. 261). Rosader was self-possessed enough to step into a tent and there indite a laudatory sonnet, which he sent to the princess in return for a jewel which she had delivered to him by the hands of a page (p. 21). The intervention of the page in the matter may account for Rosader's business-like procedure.[2]

---

[1] See what the author of *Dorothy* says concerning Rosalind's "no matter," p. xii.

[2] See *Transactions of the New Sh. Soc.*, 1880–2, pp. 30*, 31*.

When wandering hunger-stricken in the forest, he wept
and lamented that he could not die worthily, lance in hand.
The self-sacrificing love of Adam Spencer, who would
have opened his veins in order that his young master
might be nourished by his blood, roused Rosader from
despair, and sent him forth in quest of food (p. 60). No
such faint-hearted upbraider of destiny was Orlando, cheering
his drooping follower with words of confident hope and
gentle reproof, till he saw a reflection of his own undaunted
courage in the old man's looks (II. vi. 4–*ad fin.*)

In hesitating to save Saladyne from the lion, Rosader was
biassed less by a desire for revenge than by a more far-seeing
motive. He should add Saladyne's estates to his own, and
his increased wealth might incline Rosalynd to regard him
more favourably ; it being his opinion that "women's eyes
are made of Chrisecoll,[1] that is ever unperfect unless tempred
with gold" (p. 95). The cause of Orlando's wavering was
a gust of vindictive anger (IV. iii. 128–131) ; a venial fault
if we consider his provocation. Rosader's hesitation was
chiefly due to calculating, not impulsive, culpability ; and he
was unconscious of the wrong which he designed towards
Rosalynd. His derogatory estimate of her accords with
this lack of moral delicacy.

Lastly, with Rosader's eloquent professions of love we
have to reconcile the rather awkward fact that, though he

---

[1] Chrisecoll, "Chrystall? But perhaps the same as Chrysocolla,
Harrison's 'England,' p. 236." Halliwell, *Dict. of Archaic Words.*
Cotgrave gives : "Chrysocolle (Chrysocolla), Gold-solder ; Borax ; green
earth, whether artificial or mineral, as Borrais. Borrais = Borax, or
green earth, a hard and shining mineral or humour congealed in mines.
There is also an artificial one made of Rock alum, ammoniac, and other
things ; both used by goldsmiths. Borras jaune = yellow-borax, found
in gold mines, and fittest for goldsmiths."—W. A. H.

knew of Rosalynd's exile, he did not attempt to follow her, but remained at home for, we are told, "a long while," until care for his safety obliged him to depart. I cannot suppose that Orlando could have been so sluggish and unfeeling.

4. Saladyne and Oliver are more akin, and it were hard to strike the balance between them.

Sir John of Bordeaux bequeathed the largest share of his property to Rosader. Hence Saladyne's hatred sprang chiefly from avarice, and fear of being called to account for his malversations. Oliver, whose estate was subject to a legacy of " but poore a thousand crownes " (I. i. 2, 3), had no ground save envy for detesting Orlando.

Saladyne felt compunction for his brother's wrongs sooner than did Oliver, who was certainly impenitent when banished by Duke Frederick. The imprisonment which preceded Saladyne's exile awakened some sorrow, which was, however, not deep, for when questioned by Torismond as to his brother's whereabouts, Saladyne answered reservedly that "upon some ryot made against the Sheriffe of the shire, he was fled from Bordeaux, but hee knew not whither " (p. 65). In Saladyne's presence Rosader related to Gerismond all that had passed between them (p. 101). Celia and Rosalind were the recipients of Oliver's confession. Oliver would doubtless have soon revealed himself as the unnatural brother, but, in his emotion, the truth escaped him ere he had summoned resolution enough deliberately to avow it (IV. iii. 133).

Saladyne's amorous speeches to Alinda, and her replies, are recorded for us. She expressed the conventional distrust of his good faith, and bade him reflect on their inequality of birth (pp. 128–132). How Oliver wooed Celia we are left to imagine : we only learn the issue from Rosalind, who treated the whole affair with much levity (V. ii. 32–45).

Alinda's warning was not unneeded. When, on the wedding-day, the pseudo-Ganymede, having withdrawn alone and re-entered as Gerismond's daughter, was given by the king in marriage to Rosader, Saladyne, comparing his brother's splendid alliance with his own, stood "in a dumpe" till Alinda declared herself to be the daughter of Torismond ('p. 159). Celia's entrance simultaneously with Rosalind spared Oliver this test of his constancy.

Most of us have, I suspect, wondered why Celia should have fallen in love with Oliver, and regretted that she did not choose a worthier mate.[1] Saladyne's display of prowess in the struggle with the forest-ruffians commended him to Alinda; and, in saving Rosader's life, he requited his brother's generosity, and made some atonement for past unkindness. Shakspere did not ennoble Oliver by any such device.

The minor characters now remain to be considered.

[1] Swinburne writes : "That one unlucky slip of the brush which has eft so ugly a little smear in one corner of the canvas as the betrothal of Oliver to Celia."

"The actual or hypothetical necessity of pairing off all the couples" (at the end of a comedy) "is the theatrical idol whose tyranny exacts this holocaust of higher and better feelings," &c. (*Study of Shakespeare* p. 152).—[W. A. H.]

We may derive some consolation from comparing the union of Celia and Oliver with another example, in George Eliot's *Middlemarch*. If desert alone were regarded, Mary Garth should have married Mr. Farebrother, but then Fred Vincy's ruin was inevitable. Farebrother could steer his own course aright ; poor Fred could not. We may hope that under Celia's beneficent influence the rooted evil of Oliver's nature was killed, the germ of worth in him—shown by his genuine remorse —quickened, and that he came at last to deserve his good fortune.

5. Adam Spencer exceeded the Shaksperian Adam in fidelity. The former, as we have seen, was willing to sacrifice his life in order to save his master from starvation. This especial proof of devotion forms a repulsive, and possibly an unnatural, incident. Moreover, as Lodge has used it, it degrades Rosader, whose bitter lamentations caused Adam Spencer to offer such a relief.

6. Lodge's Phœbe rejected Montanus's suit " not," as she told him, " that I scorne thee, but that I hate love : for I count it as great honor to triumph over fancie as over fortune " (p. 121). The Shaksperian Phœbe expressed no abstract preference for an unwedded state.

The violence of her passion having endangered Phœbe's life, the disguised page, at Montanus's request, visited her as she lay sick in her father's house ; and, arguing the matter with courtesy and consideration,—qualities, as I have already noticed, lacking in the other Ganymede's method of dealing with an unwelcome attachment,—drew forth this confession : " . . . so deeply I repent me of my frowardnesse towards the shepheard, that could I cease to love Ganimede, I would resolve to like Montanus " (p. 145). Shakspere did not endow his Phœbe with so much sensibility. We do not gather that unrequited love affected her health ; and her feigned pity—preluded by the gracious avowal, " Why, I am sorry for thee, gentle Silvius "—was merely the flattering transition from cruelty to treachery (III. v. 86).

7. Montanus, despairing of Phœbe's life, magnanimously advised his rival to wed her. To Alinda, who said, " . . . if Ganimede marry Phœbe, thy market is cleane mard," he answered, " . . . so hath love taught me to honour Phœbe, that I would prejudice my life to pleasure her, and die in despaire rather than shee should perish for want " (p. 142).

If rewarded sometimes by a smile, Silvius could endure the
better fortune of another wooer, but his imaginative heroism
carried him no further. He told his Phœbe that he should

". . . thinke it a most plenteous crop
To gleane the broken eares after the man
That the maine haruest reapes : loose now and then
A scattred smile, and that Ile liue vpon " (III. v. 101–104)

Further, when requested to convey the fatal letter,
Montanus, we learn, " saw day at a little hole, and did
perceive what passion pinched her [Phœbe] : yet (that he
might seeme dutifull to his Mistresse in all service) he dissembled the matter, and became a willing Messenger of his
own Martyrdom " (p. 138). The like merit cannot be
attributed to Silvius, who was completely fooled.

8. Of the two shepherds Montanus and Coridon, and the
fair shepherdess Phœbe, it may be said that they are idealized
after the Arcadian model. Coridon, the prototype of Corin,
is, both in speech and ways, the most homely of the three.
Concerning Phœbe he remarked, " if al maidens were of her
mind, the world would grow to a mad passe ; for there would
be great store of wooing and litle wedding, many words and
little worship, much folly and no faith " (p. 111). Before
the wedding party went to church he presented " a faire mazer
full of Sidar " to Gerismond, with a " clownish salute "
which made the king smile (p. 150). " About mid dinner,
to make them mery, Coridon came in with an old crowd,[1]
and plaid them a fit of mirth, to which he sung this pleasant
song,

[1] A fiddle.—Nares's *Glossary*, 1867, *s. v.* See the minute description
of Coridon's " holiday sute," p. 149.

A blyth and bonny country Lasse,—
heigh ho, the bonny Lasse!—
Sate sighing on the tender grasse,
and weeping said, ' will none come woo mee?' " &c.
(p. 161).

Yet in a wooing eclogue he could warble thus to Montanus :

" This milk-white Poppy, and this climbing Pine,
Both promise shade ; then sit thee downe and sing,
And make these woods with pleasant notes to ring,
Till Phœbus daine all Westward to decline " (p. 40).

On Alinda's wedding day, Montanus " was apparelled all
in tawny, to signifie that he was forsaken : on his head he
wore a garland of willow, his bottle hanged by his side,
whereon was painted dispaire, and on his sheephooke hung
two Sonnets,[1] as lables of his loves and fortunes " (p. 151).
Touching his love he discoursed in this fashion : " Mine eyes
like bees delight in sweet flowers, but sucking their fill on
the faire of beauty, they carry home to the Hive of my heart
farre more gaul than hony, and for one drop of pure deaw, a
tun full of deadly Aconiton " (p. 151).

[1] Five other sonnets are preserved for us, one of them being in
French (p. 117). Mr. Collier said : "Lodge appears to have been
rather vain of his French compositions, and this is not the only instance
in which he has introduced them, either in his own works or as
laudatory of those of others. To put French verses into the mouth of
Montanus is a gross piece of indecorum as respects the preservation of
character."—*Ibid.*, *note.* If the forest of Arden were the forest of
Ardennes, French was Montanus's native tongue ; but since we find
Rosader and Adam journeying to the forest "through the province of
Bourdeaux," and expecting by this route to reach " Lions " (p. 56), we
are obliged to conclude that the site of Lodge's Arden is as indefinite as
Shakspere's.

Phœbe, too, had the same command of tropical language;
and her two extant sonnets (pp. 118, 137) are as pithy and
well-conceited as are the poetic fancies of the other personages
of the novel, most of whom have left us specimens of their
powers in this line.   When Rosalind and Alinda first
beheld her, she was attired " in a petticote of scarlet, covered
with a green mantle, and to shrowd her from the Sunne a
chaplet of roses: from under which appeared a face full of
Natures excellence, and two such eyes as might have amated
a greater man than Montanus " (p. 115).   Lodge may put
in the touch, " a face full of Natures excellence," but we
know assuredly that she had not the " leathern hand " which
Shakspere has not shrunk from giving to his Phœbe.

The dwellers in Shakspere's Arden are drawn from
Nature, Phœbe and Silvius marking the credible limit of
rustic refinement, while in Audrey and William the ordinary
peasant type is depicted.   Old Corin fills a place between
these two grades.

9. Of Gerismond and Torismond I have only to observe,
that the former did not possess the cheerful fortitude in
adversity which distinguished the Elder Duke ; and that the
latter, in banishing his daughter as well as his niece, showed
himself to be a more rigorous tyrant than was Duke
Frederick.

It now remains to summarize the results of this examin-
ation.

Shakspere's Rosalind and Celia may be called creations :
little more than the plot through which they moved being
borrowed from Lodge.   Shakspere gave to Rosalind the
pre-eminence that the structure of the story demanded.   Her
abundant wit was also his gift.   The chief negative change

consisted in the behaviour of Rosalind to Orlando after the wrestling-match.

The development of Orlando's character was due in a larger measure to omission and substitution. By a variation in the plot, while economy of time, a dramatic gain, is effected, the hero's unloverlike sojourn at home during his lady's exile is avoided. Again, the breaking of his tryst in consequence of a prolonged ramble is rejected. Our suspicions, that, in spite of his protests, Rosader was· but a cold lover, are rather increased when we consider his behaviour—in marked contrast to Orlando—after the wrestling-match. His despondency when menaced by hunger, and the sinister calculation which prompted him to abandon his brother and make his desertion a means of winning Rosalynd, show grave defects of character from which Shakspere's Orlando is quite free.

Instead of Saladyne's avarice, Shakspere, by changing the circumstances, substituted Oliver's envy. Lodge granted Saladyne an opportunity for repairing past injuries. Shakspere denied this to his Oliver. Our attention is solely fixed on the rescue from the lioness. Oliver's repentance is, with much dramatic effect, deferred until that crowning moment, and he is not afterwards permitted in any wise to disturb Orlando's superiority. Yet, by another slight change of circumstance, Oliver was spared the risk of falling lower in our esteem, as Saladyne did when he repented his match with Alinda.

The episode of the hard-hearted shepherdess and her lover served as an under-plot; in strict subordination to the main story. The artificial air which hangs about Lodge's swains, including old Coridon, was dispelled. The Shaksperian Phœbe was simply " fancy free " ; not a sworn vestal as was her sister of the novel. Neither did love afflict her with languishing sickness. Montanus's willingness to surrender his Phœbe to a rival was not emulated by Silvius.

To this avoidance of what may at least be called highly coloured touches should be added: the toning down of the "tyrants vaine" in Torismond; and the effacement of Alinda's offer to become the guilty Rosalynd's executioner, as well as Adam Spencer's proposed self-sacrifice, which was open to the further objection that it reflected discredit on Rosader.

Lastly, the deeds of violence which embittered the brothers' strife, the battle that raged on the verge of the forest, and the lawlessness that found a shelter in its depths, have no parallels in *As You Like It*. We can forget the malice of Oliver and the tyranny of Duke Frederick amid the peace and innocence enfolding Shakespere's Arden; cruelty and injustice range without, but may not break, its charmed circle: we can return to that primal age when the loves and caprices of simple rustic folk were the chief tokens of human passion, and dwell again where we "fleet the time carelesly as they did in the golden world."